T0209736

LIVING LIFE UNCONSCIOUSLY

A Guide To Waking Up And Living Life With Purpose

LINDSEY ZIEGLER, MA, LPC

BALBOA.
PRESS

A DIVISION OF HAY HOUSE

Balboa Press books may be ordered through booksellers or by contacting:

Balboa Press
A Division of Hay House
1663 Liberty Drive
Bloomington, IN 47403
www.balboapress.com
1 (877) 407-4847

Print information available on the last page.

ISBN: 978-1-9822-2148-5 (sc)
ISBN: 978-1-9822-2149-2 (e)

Balboa Press rev. date: 02/19/2019

Dedicated to my family.
Scott, Emma, and Bella, you teach me so much every day.
And for my dad—
without your endless love and support
I may not have found my way.

INTRODUCTION

Who among us has not struggled with depression, anxiety, obsessive thoughts or behaviors, frustrations, irritability, anger, and so on? It's okay. I have too.

What is behind those vicious cycles of intense emotions that influence our behaviors? The thoughts in our heads keep reinforcing what we have to feel sad or lonely about or what we have to worry about. What if there was a way to stop the vicious cycle for good and find lasting happiness? There is a way, and it starts with understanding those thoughts.

Through these pages, I will clearly illustrate how we can all detach from our negative self-talk, later defined as egoic thought, and take back control of our lives. This is only a piece of a greater spiritual awakening that is currently taking place in the world. Another piece to this awakening is the larger collective *knowing* that there is something greater than all of us guiding our lives in a direction by which we will understand our true purpose—if we can slow down and increase our awareness enough to notice without being tied down by those nagging thoughts, of course. With the technique of recognizing our negative self-talk or egoic thoughts and then detaching, or grounding, ourselves, we will find a greater understanding of why we are here and what our purpose truly is during this lifetime. We all have the power to raise ourselves to the height of our true potential.

I, like most people, started out completely unconscious, completely unaware of my purpose. I know it now, and I can reflect back on moments during my life where I glimpsed it—this. Right now. I had a deep feeling that I would come to a point in my life where I would "get it," despite the somewhat frequent times in my life where I felt hopelessly lost. I feel in every fiber of my being that this is so important to share. We have a purpose in our lives, and we all struggle to reveal that purpose in our lifetimes. The struggle can end if we can learn how to truly wake up and participate fully in our everyday lives. It comes as we begin to understand our thought and behavior patterns, what they are linked to, and how we have been shaped and influenced by those around us. I will get into the science and psychology behind all of this as well as outline the ways in which this can be applied to our lives to bring about lasting and positive changes.

By recognizing the negative self-talk, or egoic thoughts, we increase our overall awareness and our ability to make choices more objectively in order to move our lives forward in the direction we truly want to go. Developing the ability to recognize egoic thoughts may be slightly easier than harnessing the energy it takes to ground ourselves. Grounding is the process of narrating for ourselves what is actually happening right here and right now. Imagine pulling yourself back down to the ground, to reality. Those egoic and frequently negative thoughts have become so engrained in us that, initially, it feels almost unnatural to detach from them and pull ourselves back down to planet Earth. Instead of aligning with the egoic thoughts, however, we must recognize them and bring ourselves back to the present moment by pulling ourselves out of those thoughts and detaching from the emotional reactions that spur from them.

Leave behind you any feelings of uncertainty, nervousness, doubt, or sadness. If you are ready to learn how to move beyond the limitations of your emotional reactions to the endless chatter of thoughts in your head, then your time is now. I implore you to recognize that everything is happening at the same time, so to speak. Right now, someone may be dying while another new life is being born. There may be torrential rain affecting someone's commute as a crisp, blue sky shines for another, just as a songbird has her agenda, singing sweet music, and we have ours, with our minds full of egoic worry that need not define us, let alone set the tone for our days and our lives. I invite you to wake up and begin living your life *consciously* and with purpose.

I became increasingly interested in the idea of managing emotional reactions that influence our behaviors throughout years of professional development as a Licensed Professional Counselor. I always knew that I wanted to be a therapist, and the journey was long and arduous. In looking back, I can easily see how I went from living my life completely *unconsciously*, constantly blaming my perceived "bad luck" on the universe's conspiring against me or just being doomed in life. In moving from that unconscious state of being to coming into alignment with a higher version of myself and my life's purpose, I feel more comfortable in my own skin and am far less emotionally reactive when things don't go my way. I now choose to accept unfortunate circumstances and view them, not as bad luck, but as lessons that life is offering me on my journey. Everything happens for a reason.

It can be challenging to open up in this way. It might go against the grain, in a way. In the seemingly endless cycle of anxiety and sadness, the choice to be vulnerable enough to accept the unpleasant circumstances we find ourselves faced with may seem counterintuitive. I spent some time there too, in that vicious cycle of sadness and despair. There is a way out.

Perhaps one of the greatest lessons I have learned in my own journey is that one of our purposes in this lifetime is to remember that we are all adding to the collective growth and expansion of the world. We all have something to contribute, whether it be a beautiful piece of artwork, incredible music, a scientific discovery, or real opportunities to guide someone in some way through religion, therapy, or spirituality. We are meant for great things, and we can achieve those great things if we are truly *awake* by doing the work to look beyond our life circumstances, good and bad, in order to *remember* what it is that we are meant to accomplish. We are not meant to live in mental pain and anguish while being held hostage by our own thoughts.

This happens too frequently for many of us. When we are plagued by the worries and fears about the future or reminders of painful or embarrassing moments in our past, our thoughts are holding us hostage because we cannot move forward and are unable to live in the present moment. We, instead, are riddled with guilt and regret about something that either hasn't happened yet or that we are powerless to go back in time to change. And there we are, all the while, sitting with our minds ablaze with worry, fear, regret, panic, frustration, or any combination of intense feelings. We waste our lives, at times paralyzed by these emotions— held hostage, sitting still, or maybe pacing with only those worrisome thoughts haunting our minds. And there he is, Ego, reminding us of all of the things we have to be afraid of or worry about. But Ego's not supposed to be left in charge, and I will explain in much more detail later. We need to take back control in our lives, and I am so excited to show you how.

Briefly, this technique is the process of recognizing egoic thoughts and detaching from them by grounding ourselves in the present reality. This simple technique, practiced consistently, will help us to detach from the constant upheaval of intense emotions (worries, fears, sadness, etc.) and remain firmly planted in the reality of our present moment, freed from the emotional roller coaster. The technique will be covered in great detail in the pages to come, as will the process of how to apply it in our everyday lives. The challenges in adopting this approach are also discussed throughout because they are rooted in our psychological "hard-wiring," and, in order to change anything, we must allow ourselves to be vulnerable and honest about what it is that we want and also about how our past experiences have shaped us today.

We can choose to behave differently than we have before, and we can make the conscious effort to *think* differently once we wake up and become more aware of what is happening. This concept of rewiring is called neuroplasticity, or the brain's ability to rewire itself, and it is explained as we get into the science and psychology of our minds' inner workings. By adopting this technique and applying it to your everyday life, you will be *rewiring* your brain and changing your behavior patterns to yield different results—better results.

This will take dedication and emotional focus, and the rewards are abundant. The easier thing to do will be to do nothing at all and just allow the thoughts and emotions to have their way with you. That is the way you've been living up to this point, but it does not have to be the way you *endure* your life. No one should *endure* life; the universe does not want any of us to suffer. If you can find the strength to focus your attention differently and learn to dismiss the egoic thoughts that are ruling your life, you will, in turn, rewire your brain and change your automatic thought and behavior patterns. This will show you a different life path and a different way of living. If used consistently, through each moment of every day, you will begin to see results within weeks. But the work doesn't stop there. The challenge comes in making the conscious choice to prevent the egoic thought from running amuck and detaching from it by grounding yourself, all while living your life and tending to all of your responsibilities. That is where it gets tricky because, regardless of how mundane we may feel our lives are at times, there are so many variables that influence the directions of our thoughts. That is why we have to be consistent in our practice—you never know what life will throw at you.

Even in the wake of a crisis or traumatic experience, this technique will prove to be your tether in order to help you get through it. By remaining grounded and objective, we can make sense of it correctly, as opposed to aligning with the egoic thoughts that tend to hold us hostage in the face of adversity or conflict.

Just to offer you a little bit of history on how I got here, it may be helpful to know that throughout my own life I spent a long time battling depression and anxiety. Depression came first for me. I noticed probably around age ten as I was leaving little notes about how sad I was feeling where I was sure someone would find them. I didn't know what it was, and no one helped me figure it out. I had my first panic attack at age fifteen as I broke out in hives preparing to start my first after-school job. Again, I had no one to tell me what was happening or that I was going to be okay. From my perspective, I was growing up in a household where you didn't talk about what you were feeling and no one was there to help make sense of the emotions anyway. You just figured it out yourself. You pushed through and you figured it out. Don't talk about feeling sad or feeling nervous; that's just being dramatic. From my perspective currently, that is a reckless and cold approach to parenting. If we, as parents, have some knowledge of developing emotions and how to approach managing them, why would we choose not to share that with our children? Who knows? Maybe our parents were just as unconscious to their own emotions and pushed them aside because there were more important things to focus on.

Looking back, I was growing up with some really complex emotions, and that was my "problem." This was my perception. No one ever said that to me, but that's how I internalized the lack of open communication. At that time, I remember what I can now identify as anxiety alternating with severely depressing thoughts. I became clingy with my mother in a desperate attempt to find comfort in the complex emotions I was feeling. I didn't even know how to communicate it. I just needed someone to tell me that it was going to be okay. No one told me it was going to be okay. I stopped clinging to my mom and started to shut down, trying to figure out some other way to make sense of the emotions that I couldn't even describe. The epidemic of depression was rarely discussed. It was 1980-something, and Prozac had only just come out on the market; many were denying the fact that people suffered from depression. Back in the 80's, there definitely weren't television commercials promoting the benefits of a drug to aid anyone's mental health.

I pushed forward, despite it all; I always pushed forward. Why? I honestly wouldn't have been able to tell you at that time. I thought about suicide frequently, even turned to self-injury for a short while in middle school. No one noticed.

I grew more depressed. So I started to experiment with alcohol. Everything I did, I did with the same hope—that someone would notice and not just yell and attack but come to me and tell me they loved me and wanted to help me. At this point I was probably sixteen and my parents had been divorced for about two years. I was living with my mom until the night came when I had to leave. Then I was really alone, lost with Ego. That period of time when I was moving from friend's house to friend's couch felt like forever. The only thing keeping me company was Ego, and he never shut up. When I wasn't sure where I would be sleeping that night or if I had enough money for food, he was there narrating for me: *You're a screw-up. You messed up big time, and now you have to handle it.* Leaving home when I was sixteen felt like rock bottom. My egoic mind was on fire, narrating thoughts of hopelessness and of being unworthy of love or affection. I was on autopilot, and I felt myself careening out of control.

I moved in with my dad after what felt like months. I switched high schools to start my senior year someplace new, and I felt like I was now living someone else's life. It all happened so fast. I went through the motions, mostly numb.

Sometimes the panic attacks would wake me up out of a deep sleep. It felt like there was no end in sight. This was my life, or so I thought. One day, which I remember vividly, I was incredibly depressed about leaving home while on my break at work. Crying in the bathroom, I burnt my left forearm with my lit cigarette just to remind myself that I was alive and a real person. My mind was drowning in all of the horrible things that had happened recently when I had a thought break through all of that egoic noise. That thought was that I had a choice—I could choose to stay all messed up, or I could make my life something amazing. I could take all of this hurt and misery and use it to propel me forward into an amazing life because I deserve to live an amazing and fulfilling life. It was a loud thought that felt like it was not my own, like it came from outside of me. I have never forgotten that moment. There were still tough times ahead, but I knew that I was going to stumble toward great things.

What I really want to offer is a sense of hope. There are plenty of spiritual self-help books out there, and so many people pass them by because they are not quite ready to wake up on their journey. I can share other aspects of my life that, I hope, will only serve as a point for comparison to your own. Difficult and troubling things happen to us, and what we do with the emotions that come along with the situation, is what helps to shape our paths as we move forward. Through the toughest and darkest times, there was hope. I didn't see it then, but I felt it deep inside, that there was more. I could do more than just be a victim of my circumstances. In the deepest parts of my soul, I felt that my life was meant to do more than whatever this was.

I was still completely on autopilot and suffering from depression and horribly intense panic attacks that could last anywhere from forty-five minutes to five hours, but I *knew* that there was a reason to move forward. There were actually many hidden gifts throughout those hard times—blessings in disguise, I call them. Now, I can look back and see the lessons that I was being offered through my life experience. Now, I can call them gifts. Back then it felt like I was cursed.

It is for all of those gifts that I am writing this guide. For all of the people suffering and feeling like you are alone, on autopilot, contemplating suicide, or just feeling like you'd be better off crawling under a rock, there is a way out, and perhaps it is humanity's best-kept secret. Each and every one of us has exactly what we need to feel better, but no one has shown us how. We are fully equipped with all the tools necessary to wake up and actually enjoy each day instead of feeling like victims of our own lives.

Please believe that I still make mistakes sometimes and I am not perfect. By adding this simple technique of watching your egoic thoughts and purposefully detaching from them by grounding yourself in the right here and right now, you will feel better and more at peace. You will notice, very quickly, that each day can be so rewarding and full of promise instead of ruled by sad, negative, panicked, or fearful thoughts. Why should our lives be ruled by thoughts that we don't want to be thinking or feelings we don't want to be feeling?

What I'll offer throughout these pages are ways of looking at things a little differently so you, too, can slowly but surely find your way to a happier and more fulfilling life. Isn't that what we all want? It's yours; you already have it. All you have to do is wake up!

CHAPTER 1

Originally the ego includes everything, later it detaches
from itself the external world. The ego-feeling we
are aware of now is thus only a shrunken vestige
of a far more extensive feeling—a feeling which
embraced the universe and expressed an inseparable
connection of the ego with the external world.
—Sigmund Freud

I want to emphasize that you are not your thoughts. Maybe
you've heard that before. To take it a step further, *your
thoughts are not you*. Take a minute to let that sink in. What
does that mean? If your thoughts are not you, then what are
they? They are part of the basic psychological hardwiring of
every human being's brain. They are what Sigmund Freud
identified as Ego, the reality principle of the human psyche
that interprets the reality we are observing through all of our
senses. The Ego also mediates between the selfish, primitive
desires of the Id, the pleasure principle of the human psyche,
and the strict, almost uptight tendencies of the Super-Ego,
or the morality principle of the human brain. My main
focus is on the Ego and how it operates, but just knowing
that your thoughts do not need to have control over you

and that you are *not* the thoughts in your head is a key principle to this life-changing process. Those *thoughts* are Ego's narrations about what is happening all around us, and Ego tells us how we should feel about it. There comes a point in all of our lives when we need to detach from *egoic thoughts* and interpret reality for ourselves. Your time is now.

Ego

Here we will get into specifics regarding what the Ego is, what it is supposed to do, and why. Ego is a part of the human brain's functions, and that is why we can all relate. Our brains are hardwired to have this instinctual piece that tells us what is happening as we try to make sense of the world around us. Everyone has an Ego, but what everyone's Ego says to him or her about the external world is different. And, as explained in the introduction, it is influenced by our environments as well as our genetic predispositions. Ego is not bad. We can learn to work with it, but we need to understand it first. There is a way to take back control of your life by getting ahold of the thoughts in your head, regardless of what your Ego may be telling you.

Right here and right now, what's happening? Probably not much. You're reading a book. Maybe widen the scope for just a minute and think, right here, right now, generally in your life, what's happening? I bet that your mind just flooded with thoughts, ideas, memories, hopes, desires, and feelings. Shrink the scope again, and now, think, right here, right now, what just happened? You were thinking. You are still reading a book, but all of those thoughts and feelings that surged didn't "happen," did they?

On a large scale, I am asking you to objectively observe your life. On a small scale, I am asking you to watch every thought and choose whether you need to emotionally react to it or not. And, somewhere in between, you might be able to successfully improve the overall course of your life. Let's make the choice to wake up and start living our lives on purpose, with intention, instead of living each day feeling like victims in our own lives. You are a beautiful soul who was put on this planet, in this life, with these circumstances, all for a purpose. And that purpose is *not* to suffer needlessly.

When I asked you to widen the scope and all of those thoughts, ideas, memories, hopes, dreams, and so on came flooding into your consciousness, who did that? You did that, of course. Do you ever get lost in that? Lost in thought about your hopes, dreams, memories or fears? We all do, but we don't have to get lost if we can gain some awareness of what is happening. Right here. Right now.

We can actually learn how to keep our line of thought focused on a purpose and help guide our minds to wander less. You require nothing but a strong desire to calm your mind and find your happiness.

Earlier, I briefly mentioned that the thoughts in your head are not you, but they are your Ego. Psychologically speaking, this concept of the Ego is very important to recognize in our everyday lives. It's important because, for most of us, our Ego has been in the driver's seat.

Freud defined the Ego as the "reality principle," and its role is to balance out the "pleasure principle"—the Id, and the Super-Ego, or the "moralizing principle." From birth, the Ego's role is to interpret the world for us. We need him; he keeps us safe and helps us to learn how to keep ourselves safe. But after a while, we learn. We know not to stick our hand into open flames and to look both ways before we cross the street. The Ego will remind us of the things we should be careful about doing, saying, touching, wearing, and so on. This is when the Ego gets annoying. He just keeps on narrating the world for us. He just keeps rattling off things we should pay attention to and how we should feel about certain things. Ego has access to every emotion, and he evokes the emotions to validate that thought he offered to you. If Ego offers a thought or idea and we latch on to it, the emotional tidal wave hits us and we are trapped. But, not to worry—he will always be there, sharing his interpretations of what your friend really meant when she said that you talk too much or what your husband really meant when he said he had to work late for the fifth day in a row. Ego will have a field day telling you what everyone else's behavior means. The problem is that Ego is not a psychic. And because Ego just goes about his business of keeping us "safe," we are left struggling on a regular basis with feelings of depression, anxiety, anger, frustration, and feeling like we don't belong. What we have to learn how to do is recognize when Ego is offering up an interpretation of someone or something, immediately detach from that thought, and ground ourselves with facts like where we are, what day it is, and that we are alive and breathing.

The Ego is with us from birth, and its job is to keep us safe. Its job is also to interpret our reality for us, to help us make things make sense. We are so used to listening to it that it makes this whole idea of *not* listening to it, or detaching from it, sound crazy. But, in fact, most of us are living life unconsciously because we are running around completely aligned with our Ego. We are not aware of what's happening right here, right now, because we are so worried about that stupid thing that we said yesterday at work or we are so panicked about the possibility that our spouse is cheating or that we'll never make enough money or that we'll be fired tomorrow because of the stupid thing we said at work yesterday.

That's exhausting. But it's true, and that is how most of us are living every day of our lives. We can never hope to wake up if we aren't willing to do the work. Ego will just take over forever so we can sit back and—what? Enjoy life? No. Remember, if we sit back and let Ego drive us, it's exhausting and we are not even in control of where we are going. So, if we learn to be in the driver seat of our own lives, we can be free to enjoy our lives, free from the weight of depression and the torment of anxiety. We can just be right here, right now.

Honestly, it is emotionally draining to allow Ego to be in charge. Think of any battle you've ever had with sadness or anxiety or irritability. Lost in that *egoic* thought, you are a hostage forced to watch horrific or frustrating scenes play out in your mind's eye, with you having to contend with all of the intense emotions and physical symptoms that come along with it. It drains us. And we do what? We can admit that we are emotionally drained, but we also buy Ego's idea that it is all valid and real and true. We do not have to feel emotionally drained anymore. We can stop the thoughts from triggering the emotions, and we can stop fighting the uphill battle just to get nowhere.

Go back to breathing for just a minute. Just breathing. Everything else gets shoved in balloons, and we let them float away. Okay, now, in your head, say you are going to get a glass of water. *I'm going to get a glass of water.* That's what I call goal-directed thinking, and that's you being in charge of the thoughts in your head, controlling what's allowed in there. Allow me to break it down.

Egoic Thoughts

Let's explore the two so you can pay attention to the difference between goal-directed thinking and egoic thoughts.

The voice in your head, my head, everyone's head is Ego, and we've all been listening to him for years. Every human on the planet has this voice, and in every human on the planet, that voice is generally doing the same thing. Ego is more than the negative self-talk that we may recognize most frequently. We might recognize Ego as our "conscience" as he is trying to guide our moral compass to make the best decision in a situation, or he might even console us in times of trouble.

Ego is always narrating your life for you; always offering interpretations about someone else's intentions or reasons behind their behavior; reminding you that you should be really ticked off that it rained today because you have to cut the grass; and reminding you that you are so much better than your coworker and that's why you don't have to talk to him or her. These are your *egoic thoughts*.

But you've grown up, and you no longer need the Ego to tell you what to do or not do. You have a job and responsibilities, and you've got enough on your mind. So, are you ready to learn how to get back in the driver's seat of your own life? Because, up to this point, I'm just guessing that the Ego has been doing most of the driving. That voice might sound something like this:

> *You saw the way she looked at you; she hates you! You know that they think you're not good enough. You should probably walk the other way. He really thinks you are stupid so you should probably go and explain yourself so that he knows that you're not stupid, and then you'll feel better. You can't go out looking like that—people are going to think you're homeless.*

If any of that sounds remotely familiar, then you've got a problem—an Ego problem. It's okay. Most of us have this problem with our Ego. Let's fix it, shall we?

Egoic thoughts are insidious and sneaky. They slip into our minds from out of nowhere, and we rarely notice. We rarely notice because we have always let him talk. That's what makes this work so challenging to apply. I am asking you to go against the grain and think differently. Egoic thought is the natural, default setting of all of our brains. It is the default setting because Ego has been narrating for us since birth, and we do not recognize it when we first emerge into this world, so we don't know that we can and should redirect him. I will get into much more detail later about how Ego emerges and influences our moods and behaviors. Most of us just sit back and let Ego tell us what's up and what to do about it and how to feel about it.

Can you reflect back on your life up to this moment and recall how you have blindly followed those egoic thoughts and allowed them to direct you? Those egoic thoughts are the source of any episode of "drama" in your life. Ego is talking all the time and is constantly interpreting for us what is going on in the world. It makes sense to listen to Ego's interpretation of the world when we are young children. Ego begins to help guide us as we learn right from wrong and good versus bad and develop our personal moral compass and ethical boundaries. Ego might help us to reflect on events that already happened in order to direct our choices today. That is very helpful for children. It has a less desirable effect when we are adults.

As we grow, we learn and build on things we already know. We have the ability to retain information so that every day we know more and can eventually do more than we did in the days, weeks, and months prior. Ego helps us along the way, sort of like how training wheels help us learn to ride a bike. But eventually we take off the training wheels, and we keep ourselves upright by controlling our balance. So too, we can gently encourage Ego to step back and quiet down because we are adults and we've got this.

We can become terrorized by Ego and those incessant egoic thoughts. It might go something like this: *I can't believe that embarrassing thing happened. Everyone must have thought I was a complete idiot, and I must have looked like such a wreck to them. I am a complete wreck. I feel like a panicked mess. It's because I'm not eating healthy. I'm not a priority in my life or anyone else's. Because I am such an idiot.*

Those egoic thoughts, left unchecked, have the power to destroy us mentally. This is one origin of depression and anxiety. It starts with thoughts that trigger an emotional reaction that we have to contend with. Emotions are synonymous with feelings because we *feel* them physically—that knot in your stomach with anxiety or that heavily weighted blanket that comes with despair. Perhaps until this moment, you have felt powerless, as discussed earlier in the section, to control the chaos. Just think back to your own egoic thoughts, those thoughts that are influencing how to feel about someone else or what your day is going to be like because it started off a little rough. If we are not taking charge and detaching from those thoughts, we are lost amid the chaos of everyday life.

As you read on, take notice of your own egoic thoughts and the interpretation being offered to you. You do not have to accept that egoic interpretation. Instead, you can choose, on purpose, to stop, look at the facts, and come to your own conclusion. You can regain control over your life and the thoughts in your head when you learn how to discern between egoic thoughts that are riddled with emotions and goal-directed thoughts that are all you and usually void of emotions.

Goal-Directed Thoughts

Goal-directed thoughts are purely you. *I'm going to get a glass of water.* These thoughts are crisp, clear, and void of emotional interpretations. Goal-directed thoughts are happening on purpose with a purpose because they are really us! If I am going to get a glass of water, that's because I want it and I am deciding to do it. I'm not getting a glass of water because of how I feel about the water or because the water is going to be mad at me if I don't drink it. That would be an egoic interpretation about the water.

Now the tricky part is being aware all the time so that you are always in the driver's seat, making sure to lead with your goal-directed thinking. The ego still has a role; don't get me wrong. He's a good guy, and he means well. It's not his fault that no one passed along the memo that his job description changed when you grew up. That's what we need to do now—change the way our minds interpret and process information. Ego still has a job; he is still important. We just don't need him to interpret the whole world for us anymore. We still need Ego to help us in a real emergency to interpret what went wrong and what we should do to fix it. We do not need him to replay all of our worst memories when we have a few moments of free time.

You can increase the ease with which you employ goal-directed thinking when you take time to take a step back. Perhaps, practice remaining calm by incorporating meditation into your daily routine. I will get into the practice of meditation in much more detail later, but it is one practice that can lead to life-changing results.

Goal-directed thoughts are the result of you thinking with purpose, on purpose. As you learn the difference between egoic thoughts and goal-directed thoughts, you will be able to choose to remain goal-directed for longer periods of time. Detach from Ego, with all of his emotional interpretations, and choose to be you instead.

Mind Movies

Ego frequently plays us "mind movies," where we can so easily envision what Ego is telling us, what he is interpreting for us. We can see it happening, for example, how that talk with our boss will go on Monday and how we're going to end up without a job and living in a cardboard box. There is negative self-talk, but that's auditory; we can just hear it in our minds. But the mind movies that Ego can turn on for us are highly visual in nature. We literally picture the negative things happening. That triggers strong emotions, and we are certain that trauma or tragedy are about to strike.

Perhaps we just got word that our schedule is about to change at work. *Enter Ego.* Perhaps you can envision, picture in your mind, what that schedule change is going to look like and how it will impact your life. Ego plays for you a mind movie where you can picture yourself working different hours with different people, and maybe you are doing slightly different things. If Ego has already interpreted that schedule change as a bad thing that you don't like, then the mind movie will play out terribly and you may be able to picture yourself being so tired and lost and confused that you quit your job and lose your apartment and go back home to live with your parents.

If, however, Ego interpreted that schedule change as a good thing and you feel excited about it because maybe you've been waiting for this opportunity and your best friend works at those same hours, then Ego might play for you a mind movie where you can picture yourself being so much happier and your friendship growing stronger because you are working at the same time and have the same hours off each day.

Do you see how it all starts with an egoic interpretation that snowballs out of control into a full-blown panic? If we can practice remaining aware of egoic thought in the first place, then we can ground ourselves immediately when we catch Ego starting an interpretation, and we can remain calm, cool, and collected in the present moment instead of wasting time being held hostage by Ego's mind movie of the moment, depicting for us how tragic and terrible everything will surely be tomorrow. That "voice" in your head can set the stage for your entire day and possibly your entire week because, if you don't realize that voice isn't you, you'll just keep following it and believing everything it says.

Ego thinks he's keeping us safe because we've left him in the driver's seat but, in reality, we were probably all supposed to learn this in middle school so we could remain in control of our lives even as hormones shift and puberty approaches. Instead, the norm is just the opposite. We're just going about our lives, paying no attention at all to our minds, and then hormones shift and mood disorders (depression, anxiety, etc.) develop. Those mood disorders such as depression and anxiety can develop when Ego is left to interpret the circumstances surrounding something not going our way. There may be a chemical imbalance involved, but the primary culprit is the incessant chatter in your head. If left completely unchecked, perhaps personality disorders are forming too. Personality disorders can form in times of abuse (physical or emotional) and at times of severe stress or trauma. Over an extended period of time, if the mind and thoughts are left unchecked, the Ego is interpreting that trauma or stress and is "protecting itself" by skewing the perception of what's actually happening.

We have a responsibility to watch the thoughts in our minds and not Ego's mind movies. We have to know to do that, though. No one told me; I figured it out the hard way, by lots of life mistakes and my own personal dedication to figuring out the way my life is supposed to be. I have added, at the end, a list of books that have dramatically impacted my journey and have helped to give shape to what I am offering.

More and more people are actually talking about this struggle with depression, anxiety, and suicidal thoughts and feelings as well as growing mindful and trying to practice maintaining a calm mind. More and more people are entering therapy because they feel alienated from the world around them, and they may begin to question those egoic thoughts and look for direction in their own lives. It is much more widely accepted to go to therapy to explore alternative approaches to improving our lives than it used to be. I just think it's healthy, like going to your doctor annually for a physical or having your teeth cleaned.

With social media at everyone's fingertips, Ego is drowning in all of the possibilities of what might happen or even all of his various interpretations of what just occurred. Why? Because there's not a human standing in front of you; there's a screen of some sort. And what is Ego going to tell you about that passive-aggressive (was it passive-aggressive or was that just Ego's interpretation?) post that your "friend" just shared? You don't even have body language or tone of voice to interpret. You read words on a screen, but Ego is going to give you the worst-case-scenario and it's going to cause you to either give her a piece of your mind (by messenger, of course; you can't risk appearing like you care too much to everyone else out there) or internalize it, and Ego will tell you that it's okay, she doesn't matter, and everything is going to be fine tomorrow when you see her. Ego has lots of material to use when choosing the mind movie for you in each and every social situation, and social media and technology are not helping to curb his efforts.

I'm offering a clinically significant way to identify the Ego (that voice in your head) and appropriately and effectively detach from him. To do this, simply begin to recognize the voice that seems to always have something to say or something to show you; that is Ego. To detach from him, say to yourself, *That is an egoic thought*, and ground yourself with facts about right here and right now. It might go something like this: *Wow, I was just lost in thought. That must be the Ego Lindsey is talking about. Okay, so I caught it, and now I'll ground myself with facts, like the date. Today is Monday, October 1, and I am sitting in a chair, and nothing else is actually happening right now. I am just right here, right now.*

Ego has a purpose, but it is different now; it has changed over the course of your life. You don't have to be mad at him; he's a sweet little guy after all. We all have the ability to learn to recognize when Ego is in the driver's seat of our minds and gently nudge him, saying, *You're doing it again, buddy.* This brings us right back to center of the present moment, which is real and important.

When I first sat down to write this book, there was plenty of doubt. Ego was absolutely having a field day with me. I had so much self-doubt that I almost didn't want to do it. I heard that voice in my head saying, *What do you know? Who cares what you have to say? You are nobody important. No one is gonna care. So many people will laugh that you tried. You really are stupid for doing this. It's really gonna hurt bad when you send it to someone and they tell you that it's bad and no one will read it and you didn't "discover" anything new. Idiot.* He came right back to "my rescue" when I began the process of publication and others had my manuscript for the first time. The critiques of what to change were physically painful, and my egoic mind was telling me just to stop, to pull the plug because it was too painful and would probably just get worse. Where did my belief go? It was suddenly absent in the face of constructive criticism, but the thing I had on my side was that I was aware of it. I was objectively aware of those thoughts and the physical reaction, and I worked hard to detach from those thoughts. But they kept coming back.

My Ego interpreted for me some eye-rolling (which may not have actually happened), so I stopped telling people about it. *They all know you are not smart enough. They think it's already been done, and my book won't matter or even be published.* I have definitely had my own battle with my Ego over the years. I lived life unconsciously for a long time, and most of that time was spent battling a paralyzing panic disorder and spikes of debilitating depression. I had spent too many days completely in my head.

You don't want to go to work today. You'd feel better if you just stayed in bed where it's safe. Who knows what's going to happen? You don't know what you're doing at that job anyway. You can't tell them that; they'll laugh at you and fire you. You'll feel terrible if your boss told you how stupid you are, so hide it. Fake it. There's no point. Fuck it. No one cares about you and what you think, so stop it.

My ego was in the driver's seat, all right, and I had no idea. I had no control. I tried meds, therapy, drinking—nothing worked. After years of finding that nothing outside of me worked to ease the panic or pull me out of a depressive state, I slowly began the journey toward waking up.

It was really slow, though. I had spent so many years listening to the ego interpreting the world for me, so it was a little alarming when I first tried this stuff out myself. After years of being in my own therapy, trying every antidepressant and antianxiety med on the market, and self-medicating with alcohol and cigarettes, it was definitely strange that this worked. This method, this practice, of recognizing egoic thought and detaching from it by grounding myself in the present moment, over time, really quieted that voice in my head and calmed my anxiety to a point that it was almost nonexistent and did the same with my depression.

How could this combination of things that I mushed together actually help? After all, *you're really stupid. A million other people already know this, and you are such an asshole for thinking that you're special or that you're actually going to get this garbage published. You really should just stop.* Would you ever talk like that to someone you cared about? Then why do we so casually and frequently say it to ourselves? Perhaps this way of thinking about our egoic thoughts can help us to better control them. If we can catch Ego in action, maybe we can ground ourselves by asking ourselves if we would say that out loud to someone else. If the answer is no, then we have caught Ego in the act, and we will need to detach from those thoughts because they are not productive. Instead, those thoughts only help to keep us trapped in negativity.

If you are just beginning to recognize that voice, *congratulations*! You are also on your way to waking up!

Lindsey Ziegler, MA, LPC

Ego Loves Making Assumptions

We should do our best to stop assuming in general. Why? When you assume, you make an ass of you and me. Get it? Ass-u-me. Do you know who really loves to assume? Ego! He can be a real jerk when it comes to interpreting others' facial expressions or tones of voice, and he will force his perspective on us, especially when things are left unsaid by one party or another. Here is an example: I was not doing my own Ego work one day recently, and he got the better of me. I was out to lunch with my family, and my five-year-old daughter was being a challenge in ordering food she liked. I played right into it, as many of us do, without even knowing it. I was not *conscious* of it. Anyway, she was playing with her food, and I was being a nag. Oh, I admit it! I was really acting childishly, and who was there to see it, and say nothing, but my mother-in-law, whom I love dearly, but that doesn't matter to Ego and his assumptions that she would judge me harshly. However, without getting too personal, I know I have a "mommy complex" due to a bad relationship with my own mom. So, here comes Ego with all of his interpretations, which, by the way, are really just assumptions or a guess about everything. So, my daughter was playing with her food, and I was being an unconscious nag, harping on her for being picky. My mother-in-law passed a glance, and that was it. She offered to help my daughter eat a few bites, and she did. But Ego held onto that glance for the rest of the day. Oh, and he had a field day with the interpretation of that passing glance from my mother-in-law. He went on for the rest of the day saying things like, *She knows it's not a big deal that Bella's not eating. Why are you making it such a big deal? You are so overdramatic, and this is why you're a shit mom. You are fucking up your kids left and right, and this is exactly how. You make a big deal out of nothing, and you are not nurturing at all. You are so hypercritical that you know your kids are going to end up all messed up. She knows it. She saw it, and she probably feels bad for your husband and for your kids that they have to deal with you and your mood swings.*

Yeah, that was my ego all day long. I was aware of him enough to not listen and not let him take more away from my day, but he definitely planted seeds, which I took and shifted the way I looked at what happened. No, I did not say anything to my mother-in-law, but I did offer an apology to my daughter. I explained that I just wanted her to eat so she wouldn't be hungry, and I apologized for picking on her. She apologized too, and we hugged it out.

If I had not known what I know about Ego and his assumptions, I could have very easily reacted to my mother-in-law and told her that I knew what she was thinking about me and I didn't appreciate it. And I would have based it all on Ego's interpretation of her facial expression as she passed that glance during my nit-picking exchange with my daughter. My potential reaction to my mother-in-law's passing glance would have been based on nothing more than a look that Ego took and ran with, forming all of his assumptions. None of it would be based on fact or anything that was explicitly communicated to me. Ego loves to create assumptions, and so many of us just go with it because the emotion is triggered and it just feels like it all adds up. The key word there is it *feels* like it all makes sense. Are we really living our lives blindly following emotional impulses?

I had myself convinced for a moment that my mother-in-law was judging me and that I was a terrible person. It was fleeting only because I immediately did the work. I took an objective perspective and recognized what was actually happening. It was a thirty-second exchange between myself and my daughter. My mother-in-law offered some welcome assistance, which worked, and Bella was eating and everything was fine. That is what was actually happening in that moment. If I hadn't done the work to keep Ego in check, then I could have held onto that assumption that my mother-in-law thinks I'm a horrible mother, and assumptions like that have the potential to fester and grow into resentment and feelings of inadequacy. And because of what? A glance?

While this is an example from my own recent life, I hope it shines a light on Ego in action. Things like this happen to us all the time—every day for most of us. And it's so challenging. This is where grounding is extremely important. We have to take responsibility for ourselves and especially for the thoughts in our heads. We have no control over anyone else but ourselves. Up to this point, you have, perhaps, been living your life on autopilot because Ego was driving. He was interpreting everything, and that was triggering all sorts of emotions. It all seemed valid because the thought lined up with the feeling, and then there were the reactions, either behavioral or emotional. And then Ego keeps going with all of his assumptions about what the other people involved must have been thinking, feeling, saying, or doing. We have to take responsibility instead of saying things like, "Oh, that's just the way I am" or "That's just the way my mind works." Really? *That's just the way your mind works?* No. Step up and take some ownership over your *mind* and of your life and stop blaming it on things you perceive are out of your control. I am showing you how to get back in the driver's seat of your own life so you can regain your power and your purpose. Not only do we need to wake up and start living our lives consciously and on purpose, but by practicing these techniques and making them our everyday way of life, we can begin to live our lives *on* purpose and *with* purpose.

Once we know how to identify the difference between egoic thoughts and goal-directed thinking that is grounded in reality, we can begin the work of detaching from those egoic thoughts and spend our time more productively and less absorbed by Ego's mind movies. Dismissing those egoic thoughts as they come up, time after time, and practicing remaining grounded in the right here, right now, helps us react to what we need to react to, which, more often than not, is nothing. Right here and right now, what do you need to be having any emotion about? Why are you feeling a certain type of way, right now? Right now, I am feeling uncomfortable because I have heartburn. That discomfort is leading to mild amounts of frustration, but not at anyone or anything besides the heartburn. That's it. However, left unchecked, that heartburn could lead to frustration that I may take out on my kids who are currently playing in the other room. And if that had happened, you know, as the objective audience, what would that make me? A horrible person? An "unconscious" person? Objectively, you can see that if I was just more aware of what was happening within my own body, I could change my reaction. And, as the objective audience of this tiny aspect of my life, do you see the two paths that lay before me? Those same two paths lay before all of us all the time. But you have to know about it in order to take the other path, the path toward less struggle and strife, the path toward peace and serenity. It's really very simple once you get the hang of it. If you can see these paths as I illustrate aspects of my life, please apply them to your own life. Notice yourself making a knee-jerk reaction to something and be vulnerable enough to own it. Stop yourself as soon as you catch it and change it. Change your reaction and own that you were driven by emotion and that your Ego was driving that emotion because he fuels you with assumptions.

This takes practice because, while much of our daily routine may feel monotonous, there are tiny little variants that affect us each day. These are the things we need to be awake for and aware of so we truly see them and are not besieged by them. One tiny variant could be that you overindulged last night, and that led to your waking up with heartburn, which can lead to frustration. True story, I overindulged last night, and yes, that's why I have heartburn today. I have a wicked addiction to frozen pizza. That was my dinner after I got the kids to bed. Yes, it was nine o'clock. Yes, I know that is way too late to eat a heavy meal. I know, but I did it anyway. And perhaps that frustration leads to your reacting with road rage a bit as you are on your way to work the next morning.

And this road rage gives Ego lots of material to work with, so he will start interpreting for you why *these people are driving so slowly and that they should not be permitted on the road at all, especially if the speed limit is forty-five and they're only going forty. Seriously, it's just a suggestion, and you have someplace you need to be*!

Left unchecked, Ego takes over with ease, as is evidenced by my egoic rant in that example. My Ego was interpreting what the reaction would have been had I been presenting this information to a live audience. Right here, right now, I am sitting in my pajamas at my dining room table at 8:43 a.m. on Monday, March 19. There is no reason for me to feel judged or frustrated or anything other than content.

Let's take this information one step further and apply it to the disease of addiction. I am not a professional addictions counselor, but I have witnessed the devastating effects addictions can have on people and their loved ones. I have also lost friends to the darkness of addiction. This information about ego and fighting to regain our power to take our rightful place as *us* in our true forms can and should be applied to the battle against addiction. And I'm talking about addiction to anything and everything. Whether it be an addiction to online shopping, caffeine, alcohol, or pizza, this technique of recognizing egoic thought in action and grounding ourselves with facts relevant to the present moment can be taught and put to use in an instant. We have to be willing, and that's where the psychology comes into play. Why do some who may be suffering appear unwilling? Because it's hard. Because it's a challenge to devote mental focus and mental energy to making ourselves *think* differently. In the case of addictions, the Id (the pleasure principle) is more powerful than the Ego, but they are both battling for their turn in the driver's seat of your life.

Freud defined the Id as the pleasure principle in our brain's hardwiring, and it can be very impulsive. He just wants what he wants when he wants it. Ego, as the reality principle, is trying to get Id under control. This is true for all of us, but in the case of addictions, the Id is bigger than the Ego. Id wants the next thing, the next drink, the next slice and if we are not *aware*, we fall back on excuses that we are somehow powerless against ourselves. Seriously, and I know it might sound a bit harsh, but isn't that what we are saying when we don't take responsibility for our actions? Instead of being victims of our own lives, let's stand up, own all of our faults, take responsibility for them, and move forward today by making a few different choices for our lives. Let's start today the process toward waking up so we can begin to live our lives consciously and on purpose, with purpose. We are not victims of things that happen to us; we are victims of laziness by holding steadfastly to the belief that life happens to us and we are powerless to change our circumstances. It might *feel* that way, but by taking an objective perspective once we are grounded in reality, we may see things differently.

It's All a Matter of Perspective

Visualize climbing a mountain, and once you reach the top, you can see now what is below you. You can see the buildings, the tiny homes, the streets, and the grid where you live your everyday life. Now, imagine climbing up that same mountain but from the opposite side. You get to the top and look down, and yes, you still see the grid where you move from point A to point B every day, but from this side, from this *point of view*, you can see the reason there is traffic—it's due to a tree that is down. Perhaps you can see the flow of traffic follows a path that everyone is powerless to change because it has existed for so long and the grid, with all of the buildings and homes, was built around it. From this perspective, perhaps you can begin to understand that if you were one of those tiny cars down there, there's no reason to be flipping out because everyone is doing the best they can to follow the path that they have no choice but to follow. You have no reason to flip out about the things you cannot change.

It is all a matter of perspective. While you were on top of your mountain, things about where you live and work looked different, right? The reason we need to take time to ground ourselves in reality by gaining some perspective is so that we can react to what is actually happening instead of reacting to emotions and emotional interpretations from our ego. Before you climbed the imaginary mountain, you may have been sitting in your car, yelling at the cars in front of you because *they don't know how to drive and you have someplace important to be and rabble, rabble, rabble, grrrr.* That seems pretty silly now as you stand on top of Ol' Smokey, doesn't it? Zoom in to see that angry dude screaming about all sorts of stuff he has no control over. Zoom out, by gaining some objectivity from an objective perspective, and you see that the flow of traffic will resume once the downed tree is moved. So, what is there to freak out about? If that angry dude was able to "zoom out" and recognize that the real reason he was feeling mad and frustrated by the traffic was because he was late getting out of the house because he was obsessively checking his hair, and then zoom out further to see that it was Ego who was fueling that by saying something like, *Your hair looks stupid and if you go to work with stupid hair then Sally is never going to take you seriously if you ask her out because she's going to think, Geez, Dick really has stupid hair and I don't want to be seen with him and his stupid hair.*

And there we have the full circle. Ego plants seeds that we so willingly allow to take root in our minds, and we blindly (unconsciously) follow them anywhere they go. Sounds pretty dumb. So, do you wanna wake up now? When you feel like life is working against you, please climb the mountain, gain some perspective, and look at what's actually happening.

Ego and Trauma

I truly believe that all of us have experienced or will experience some form of trauma throughout our lifetimes. I am not saying this to rain on your parade, but it's a fact that bad things happen. Now, my trauma may look very different from your trauma, and someone may misinterpret getting a flat tire for trauma. The definition of *trauma* is "a deeply distressing or disturbing event; or physical injury." Clearly there is room for interpretation there. The fact remains, especially after looking at that definition, that at some point in our lives, we will experience a deeply distressing or disturbing event.

When trauma occurs, we need support. We may benefit from talking about it and how much it hurts emotionally and physically, especially if we can find someone who has been through the same thing or something similar. And those things might take some of the edge off for a little while, but we can use those moments of release to do the real healing work of detaching from those egoic thoughts and grounding ourselves in reality, in right here and right now and in the things that we are grateful for having in our lives. Those can be sobering facts—those things we are grateful that we actually do have. Ego spends a lot of our time going on and on about what we don't have and why we don't have it. And, seriously, what does he know?

I'll offer an example of an extremely traumatic event: a young woman miscarries her first child. And it's an extremely traumatic event because it is sudden and unexpected, and there is nothing anyone can do about it. It happens to many women and some handle it better than others, but it is a trauma nonetheless.

How does one come back from a loss like that? Well, I am sure that Ego would most likely have a blast with that situation if you were not already practicing Ego detachment, grounding, and employing positive affirmation and perspectives. In this situation, the young woman will need to heal—deeply physically and emotionally heal. But, how do you heal something that is not visible to the naked eye?

When traumatic things happen to us or we witness traumatic things happening to others, our Ego is there, interpreting. Usually it goes something like this: *Why me? Why would this happen to me? What did I do to deserve this? What if I can never have children? What is my life going to be like without being able to have a family? I have always wanted a family, right? Yeah, I think so. My husband is definitely going to leave me because he made it clear he wanted a family, and he did not sign up for a childless marriage. This was always the plan. My body is defective in some way. I must have done something to screw up my body so that I can't have kids. It must have been that stupid sandwich I ate the week before the miscarriage. The doctor said no deli meats, and did I listen? Nooo, of course not. I never listen. I'm so stupid. I'm so selfish.*

This poor woman is lost in egoic thought, lost in her own mind, while trying to make sense of this tragic event. Ego will not help her or anyone faced with a trauma. Ego has only the power that we give him. Lost in thought is no place to sort out tough stuff, but maybe getting lost in thought is a little easier than having to face the reality and trying to move forward.

Even in the face of traumatic events, we can pull ourselves out of the pit of despair if we only know how. If we know, we can at least attempt to combat those thoughts with grounding facts and truth. But through darkness, we can choose to find the positives. They are there, and there is great power in the ability to cultivate positive thoughts in the face of unpleasant circumstances.

There Is Power in Positive Thinking

The silver lining is always there, and we can find it if we can sort through the blurry emotions that cloud our perspective. There is great power in the ability to cultivate positive thoughts in the face of unpleasant circumstances.

The power-of-positive-thinking movement itself has been increasing in popularity since the late nineteenth and early twentieth centuries in North America. Our minds are incredibly powerful, and we would be wise to learn how to harness our own power. I believe the power lies, partly, in our ability to reframe our circumstances and find some slightly more positive perspective. We can do this when we are grounded, when we detach from the egoic thoughts that influence us, and when we choose to stand tall in the face of uncertainty.

This only comes after we've spent time practicing our ability to detach from egoic thoughts by grounding ourselves in the right here, right now. The influence of positive thinking is incredibly powerful, but up against Ego, it is difficult to predict a winner. If we can resolve to maintain our objective and grounded perspective, despite the curveballs that life may throw our way, we can employ positive reframing, or taking a positive point of view, to our advantage. Finding the positive in any situation will never yield bad results.

I am not encouraging delusional thinking or denying reality for what we prefer, but rather looking straight at the cold, hard, oftentimes uncomfortable situation in front of us and finding a positive way to understand it. For example, you've got a deadline at work coming up, but your four-year-old has not been sleeping through the night and is subsequently getting you out of bed several times throughout the night. You are exhausted, with limited patience for your family since your livelihood depends on making this deadline successfully. Ego gains strength when we are physically or emotionally exhausted or if we are battling a medical illness, so in this situation, your ability to remain grounded may be severely limited. And your ability to focus on your work is also diminished due to lack of restorative, REM sleep. You have choices, as you always do, and in this situation, I would encourage just a ten-minute meditation to gain even a small amount of clarity. During this short meditation, you will hopefully find success in detaching from that egoic interpretation that already has you certain of failure and that your family will soon be scrounging for food and living in a cardboard box. Then, after recognizing that feeling of serenity, you can ground yourself even further by *positively affirming* for yourself that you will be successful in meeting your deadline. *Slow and steady wins the race.* And "this too shall pass" with your young child because they are still so young and just trying to figure it all out themselves. No need to allow your little one's sleeplessness to define your future. Is it frustrating? Yes. Are you tired? Yes. Are you still just as capable as you've always been? Absolutely! This is just a moment in yours and your little one's lives. It's all right. The world is not ending, and those egoic thoughts are not prophesying your future. They are just giving you something to think about—or something to worry about unnecessarily because you are not a psychic foretelling the future, and neither is Ego.

By using the power of positive thinking to your advantage, you can calm your mind, quiet those egoic thoughts, and recognize the power you have over fulfilling your life's purpose or just finishing your work to meet your deadline! By increasing your ability to detach from egoic thoughts, grounding yourself through meditation or just conscious effort, and employing the power of positive perspectives, you can begin to regain control over the direction of your life as well as the influence your emotions have over you, even when things do not go your way.

Ego in a Real Crisis

This may be the only time that we still need Ego once we are functional adults—when there is a true crisis or emergency. Since Ego's job is to keep us safe, he will be interpreting what is going on around us to help us makes sense of everything. In the event of a crisis, like a car accident, for example, we need Ego to narrate for us what we need to do. And he's there for us, immediately, because he's always working. Somewhere in the midst of the crisis, we might feel paralyzed by fear or pain, but Ego is there reminding us of what just happened and what we should probably do next. Most of the time he's just assessing the situation for us, and then he breaks in with his interpretation of what to do next. A bit later, he might chime in with why it happened, and that is when we have to catch him and redirect our minds.

There are times where Ego may interpret your emotional response to anxiety, which only perpetuates your anxiety. For example, if you are feeling nervous and Ego begins to scan for information so he can tell you why you are anxious, the simple act of allowing Ego to interpret your emotional state makes it worse. Ego does this because your emotional reaction mimics a crisis. You may be feeling so nervous that Ego thinks he's got to tell you what's up and what to do about it. The trick is recognizing all of that and detaching from him as quickly as you can.

Left unchecked, he might interpret a situation that happened that wasn't your fault, but maybe he'll tell you it was. Maybe he'll tell you a combination of both and you will believe it. And what is his interpretation based on? Fact? Not really. In this situation, we would benefit from grounding ourselves and just reacting to what we have to do next. We can really do without all of the extra chatter.

As we continue to allow Ego to interpret our reality and every aspect of our day-to-day lives, we actually get lost. In a crisis or a traumatic situation, where we need him to help us out, most of us don't know how and when to turn him off and turn him back on again.

So how do you work through it, either way—whether it was an incorrect egoic interpretation or a fact that Ego wouldn't let you forget? It begins with awareness. We have to wake up and achieve some level of awareness in order to recognize that something is wrong. Something is wrong either with the way you are thinking or with you emotionally. And then you find yourself a good therapist and start unraveling your journey in order to understand where you've been and where you are going and decide if that is truly where you want to be. Once you achieve some level of awareness that something's got to give, you can begin to wake up. Face the demons that you hold onto so tightly and challenge them. Challenge them because they are probably rooted in egoic thought and are no longer relevant in your life. Perhaps those demons were rooted in egoic interpretation and you need to challenge them in order to help Ego recognize that he is an overachiever and hand him his updated job description, which highlights that he is predominantly necessary in a *true* crisis.

Once you can recognize that these concepts are real and you can actually take back your life, I hope you feel empowered to do so. You no longer have to bear the cross of what happened to you in your life. Gone are the days when you just blame it on the way your brain works or the way you are. You can actually begin to move through life with less worry and fear of being judged or criticized.

Here is a tiny social experiment I did while adding to this book. No lie—I have never eaten in a restaurant alone. I was afraid of how I would be perceived by others. I was afraid I would be looked at strangely and judged. That's why I never did it. It would be such an uncomfortable feeling to have Ego all but screaming at me that I would be silently labeled as weird or some kind of reject by sitting alone and eating. Maybe there is some residual middle school or high school association linked to this fear. I know, for me, that whom you sat with or were seen talking to in the lunch room at school could have a very severe social impact on the rest of your school year. Regardless, I never really gave much thought to the idea of dining alone until I really got into the work of detaching from the egoic thoughts that had been steering the direction of my life. Once I became fully aware of Ego, I challenged myself to debunk this irrational fear. And, I swear to you, as I write these words, I am currently in a busy restaurant at lunchtime. In between bites of my veggie burger and a couple of fries, I write on. I was all locked up with egoic thought driving an intense fear prior to committing to the decision to do this.

They're going to look at you weird. Everyone there is going to think, "What's wrong with that girl. She must have no friends." Is the waitress going to take pity on me and try and be my friend? Will I have to stay looking busy so people know that I'm actually doing something? Would I just be more comfortable if I went home? It's gonna feel too weird.

Why? I am here, and I am so glad I came. I was nervous right up until I got out of my car. So nervous, in fact, that I interrupted the waitress who was greeting me by blurting out my order. I was so nervous I could have made the embarrassing thing I so feared come true. But I know Ego's many tricks, and I caught him as he was attempting to interpret the situation for me. I stopped him in his tracks, and I was grounding myself for the remainder of my lunch break. And do you know what? I thoroughly enjoyed my lunch and my time at lunch. Why should I care what anyone else thinks about me, here or anywhere else? I didn't know anyone there, and even if I did, I was not doing anything strange. *Thanks, Ego. I'll take it from here.*

The other benefit of writing at a busy restaurant is that it gave me an opportunity to be present for some other people's egoic presence. What I mean by *egoic presence* is the way people speak to each other and what they are saying to each other—people talking about other people, about how much better they are than those other people. They talk about how much they know and how much they have achieved.

Armor—it is all armor that we wear to prove that we are okay, and we've earned the right to be okay in our lives. This is perhaps the origin of bullying. There are several origins of bullying, but perhaps this is another one. We put others down, either to their faces or behind their backs, to make ourselves feel better. *Ego*—he is the one doing it, and we go with it and own it as our own.

How many bullies have we heard about in recent years who have grown up, recognized that they were wrong, and gone back and apologized to those they bullied? And how many never become so humble as to realize they were wrong? Startling numbers. Our Egos are so fragile, which makes us so fragile. This, in turn, makes us feel that we can't do so many things in our lives, which, again, in turn, leads to our relying on Ego to tell us the way it is. We have never been in control of our own lives, and to take control feels scary. We almost find ourselves relying on Ego to just do it for us. It's too difficult to do this work by ourselves.

CHAPTER 2

A story has no beginning or end: arbitrarily one
chooses that moment of experience from which
to look back or from which to look ahead.
—Graham Greene, *The End of the Affair*

How Did We Get This Way?

Our lives are all a matter of perspective—what we choose to
see and how we choose to see it. Let's get into understanding
the concept of waking up and ways in which you are not
currently awake or aware of what you have control of today.
What I mean is living your life on purpose and with purpose.
You might think you are already doing so, but I encourage
you to read on. Throughout this chapter, we will learn how
our thoughts frequently attempt to undermine what we
truly want to accomplish and how the emotional reactions
that erupt from those thoughts really complicate things.
We will recognize those thoughts and detach from them
by remaining aware and awake and making more objective
decisions. I want to give you back control of your life.

Waking up isn't easy to do. Figuratively and literally, most of us struggle to wake up for work or school, and this deeper, psychological waking up is not easy either. It requires nothing of you but your ability to focus some mental energy on choosing to think differently. I find it to be a rather frightening thought that many of us could be living our lives unconsciously—literally, living life unconsciously by feeling powerless against the thoughts in our own minds. We are living life on autopilot.

I talk about waking up day in and day out in my work, but I felt that I had to share this with a wider audience because many of us are not fully participating in our own lives. Living life unconsciously is an epidemic that few even know exists. The root of this epidemic lies, perhaps, in the human history of denying emotions and focusing on survival. In order to wake up, start with understanding mindfulness and the importance of each moment. There is so much more to it than just paying attention to right here and right now. We have to understand the psychological purpose of the Ego and how and why we need to detach from it in order to be free to explore our true potential.

Controlling the Chaos

We also have to understand what we have control over in our daily lives, while it may feel that we have control over nothing. Perhaps the universe seems random to us because we do not have access to the map that it's following. But everything happens for a reason, so it's "written" somewhere. We just don't know about it, this plan for our lives. But Ego is narrating for us always, which leaves us feeling as though we should know what's going to happen next.

When we find ourselves struggling with depression, anxiety, frustration, or anger, there are ways that we can help ourselves if only we could pay attention to this exact moment and realistically what is happening right here and right now. Our ability to slow things down and shrink the scope of what we are allowing in our minds is within us all. In this very hectic, overwhelming, and overly connected world, slowing down may seem like a luxury you cannot afford, but it is perhaps a necessary evil in order to maintain our sanity. The more chaotic your life feels, the stronger the indication that you have to slow down. Especially in times of trouble or emotional struggle where we may feel powerless in our own lives, we must find the strength to resist the temptation to give in and instead take a step back.

We may not be able to control what happens to us, but we always have control over how we react or respond to what is happening. Reacting or responding appropriately and correctly, however, requires an accurate understanding of what is actually happening, which is difficult to maintain. Our emotions have been dictating how many of us live our lives, and every emotion is linked to our thoughts. We don't need to control our thoughts, per se, but instead we would be wise to be much more discriminatory regarding which thoughts we allow to occupy our headspace. That is something we all have control over, but we rarely exercise that authority.

In the Moment

Be aware of this moment only. Right here, right now, what's actually happening? I'm sitting at my desk typing. There is nothing else. It's peaceful and tranquil, and it can be like this all the time, as long as I am dedicated to practicing. It takes practice to stay here in this peace and calm. This is how we can begin to control which thoughts we allow ourselves to be influenced by, thereby averting any feeling of powerlessness in our lives. I'll explain.

In the beginning, we are born. Our minds are preprogrammed with a few tendencies that emerge as we age, but the rest is based on experiences and our surrounding environments. Ever heard of the nature-versus-nurture debate in psychology? Well, this is it in action. *Nature* is what we are genetically preprogrammed for or predisposed to, while *nurture* refers to the environment around us; our parents' temperaments and tendencies; our siblings; those who care for us; and those who ignore us, physically abuse us, or emotionally abuse us. Our minds develop based on external factors and those internal factors with which we were preprogrammed at birth. Everything combines over time to shape who we are, how we see every day, and how we see the world at large. Optimism and pessimism, for example, are perspectives that we choose to adopt in our lives because Ego tells us they suit us. I'll explain. The optimist is, perhaps, shaped by his surroundings and can find the "bright side" in most situations because he saw it in most people around him growing up and had the chance to practice it himself. He was probably encouraged to use optimism to his advantage, and so Ego would incorporate that into his daily narrative of the world around him. The pessimist, on the other hand, wasn't so lucky. She may have grown up in an environment where times were tough, and she knew it because everyone was always talking about it. The pessimist may have been surrounded by grumpy people with a grumpy outlook on life. You don't look at the bright side because, she was told, *How do you find a bright side in your father being laid off from work and your mother having to work three jobs? Life is nothing more than hard work and suffering until you die.*

It also shapes our tendencies to develop depression, anxiety, or worse, a personality disorder. For example, if we have a skewed perception of other people, that perception can be generalized to include everyone—a developing personality disorder. A narcissistic personality disorder may develop if an individual is inappropriately shrouded from the world and only given the parent's or loved ones' perspective that that individual is perfect and can do no wrong. This person may then continue through adolescence to have a sense of entitlement because, well, how could he not? If you are told for your whole life that you are perfect and everyone else is wrong in some way or another, then wouldn't you believe it? Especially when others dislike you or treat you poorly? The default for this person may be that those others are just jealous because they are not him. Narcissists think they are the greatest thing in the world because they've been raised to think (which Ego continues to reinforce) and feel that they are perfect. Don't try to bring it to their attention; they'll only look at you like you have five heads. It won't make sense because it goes against all of that original programming.

An antisocial personality disorder may more commonly be linked to the idea of a psychopath or sociopath. These individuals' personality disorders were more likely rooted in trauma and harsh circumstances, or they can be completely genetic or neurochemical in nature. An antisocial personality disorder is present when individuals have no care for others and no remorse and they'll do what suits them no matter what the cost is to anyone else. They do not care about you or anyone else. They live only for themselves, possibly because they grew up under harsh or abusive circumstances and that is what was reinforced to them by those around them. Life is harsh and cruel, and you have to do you because no one else cares. Or, if the disorder is purely chemical in nature, they may have grown up surrounded by love and affection, but the genetic hardwiring pushed them toward a more harsh and cynical way of looking at things, and Ego only helped by narrating that perspective. In a way, we are what our Egos tell us we are, until we get older and we have the choice of how we look at things and in what ways we choose to react. Our Egos start to narrate what we observe and then pull from the genetic predispositions to shape who we are and where our moral and ethical lines are drawn.

This is when you develop your assumptions, like, *That girl is really pretty. She's probably mean.* And those assumptions translate into how to behave around people you perceive to be pretty. This is just one example, of course, and our minds develop many of these assumptions based on actual experiences or even situations that we observe, whether it be on television, in the mall, or at work.

Cut to present day, and just imagine how many assumptions you've collected! And do you remember why you should never assume? It makes an ass of u and me. Don't do it. We should never assume anything.

Psychologically speaking, your assumptions have actually caused you to develop defense mechanisms that, in part, shape your personality. Some people become incredibly sarcastic and kind of mean as a defense to keep people at arm's length, for whatever reason. By developing these assumptions and defense mechanisms, many of us find ourselves all twisted up inside with anxiety and fears about what others think, or maybe we're all weighted down with depressive thoughts and beliefs about why we are not worth anyone's time or attention.

We all have our own circumstances, and we do not need to live as though we are victims of our circumstances. And, yes, sometimes shit happens. Sometimes bad things happen to good people, and those things, too, shape our perceptions of the outside world. And we take those perceptions with us everywhere we go, encountering people every day and interpreting their behavior based on all of those previously stored assumptions and your own individual defense mechanisms. Maybe we turn cynical and judgmental toward other people. Maybe we shut out the world completely because bad things have happened to us; *What's the world ever done for me anyway?* Well, that, my friends, is where the work begins. In that moment where, perhaps, we are making the choice to shut out the world because the world hasn't been there for us, the thing driving that thought is actually called the Ego. I'll get into that in more detail, but it's important that you begin to understand how your and my and everyone's minds develop and how we all develop specific behaviors associated with those idiosyncrasies. And those behaviors affect us and those around us. The more important piece here is that behind all of that are our thoughts.

Our thoughts are always with us. That's where we get the phrase "train of thought"; it's always running. Our thoughts are shaped by everything we've just mentioned—our experiences, our assumptions, and our defense mechanisms. Our thoughts get into this never-ending cycle that is constantly interpreting the world around us. Thoughts get shaped into assumptions, which add to our defense mechanisms, which trigger emotions and solidify into our perception—how we generally look at the world around us.

As I noted in the introduction, you are not your thoughts. You are the one who is aware of the thoughts. In a way, you are the watcher, or the observer of the thoughts. These thoughts are the result of years of conditioning—programming, if you will—that influences your every move, reaction, and mood. Thoughts do not define you, and they should not dictate who you are as a person. For example, I, Lindsey, am not the things I think. I am Lindsey. I am not the thoughts that tell me, *You're really lame, Lindsey, for thinking you can write a book. You're really full of yourself, and you don't know anything that everyone else in the world doesn't already know. You should stop talking about it because when they realize that you could never get published, they're going to know that you're full of shit. The jig is up. You're a complete screw-up. Just like everything else in your life, you will mess it up.*

That's not me. Those are some pretty mean thoughts, though, right? It happens. And sometimes it happens a lot. It probably happens to you too. It's okay. We're not abnormal. Just the opposite—we are so normal, I think this is the normal human condition. This is what all of our minds do, and now we know a little bit more about why and how our minds get shaped the way they have.

So what do we do about it? We reel it in, of course. We get ahold of ourselves and snap out of it by applying the technique of recognizing egoic thought and detaching from it by grounding ourselves in the right here, right now and what is actually happening. Watch the thoughts and recognize they are egoic thoughts that are telling you what must be happening or how others must be viewing you. Detach from those thoughts and ground yourself with facts. It's Tuesday, July 10, and the sun is shining as I'm sitting at my desk typing. That's all that's happening right now, so that's all that I need to react to—not the incessant chatter in my head that is also evoking a storm of turbulent emotions that I have to physically deal with. We have to learn to be kinder to ourselves, especially when we adopt this technique and begin to reprogram our minds on purpose the way we want them to be. One way that we can begin to be kinder to ourselves is by learning how to let go of our past. It's okay. It happened. Maybe bad things happened, but it's okay now. Those thoughts of past hurts, wrongs, injustices, or mistakes frequently taint the present moment because Ego won't let you forget them. And they become intrusive, unwanted, negative self-talk that we feel like we cannot escape. Detach from those egoic thoughts and ground yourself in right here and right now because that is what is actually happening. Whatever happened, happened; all you can do now is learn from it and rise above it in order to move forward and away from those things that may have defined you.

How many of us are blissfully unaware of those thoughts in our heads? Then we need to get to work to increase the level of awareness so we can get back in control of the direction our lives are headed. On the other hand, how many of us are walking around on autopilot with thoughts like that basically driving us and our actions, our behaviors, and our perceptions? Probably a lot more than we'd like to admit. But for those, please take some solace in the fact that you are already aware. You've probably been aware for a while, but you were being held hostage by your thoughts. They were driving your emotions and, hence, your behaviors, thus dictating the direction of your life. That's so frightening— the idea that many people we all encounter on a daily basis are completely driven by that endless train of thought instead of an actual purpose or goal.

Really think about that train of thought going on and on about everything. *It's really windy out today. That's annoying because I just raked the leaves yesterday. I'm hungry. I didn't have breakfast. I shouldn't eat anyway. I have to lose twenty pounds. I'm so fat. So embarrassing. Now I just feel depressed. What's the point? Twenty pounds is a lot.*

What was that? Geez, that train of thought started with the freakin' weather! How did it get all the way to how fat you are and even to affecting your mood? You got depressed about what? Your thoughts? Exactly! When left unchecked, our thoughts are dictating everything, and we don't even notice. Or maybe we notice, but we make the common mistake of believing those thoughts are us. We mistakenly believe the thoughts in our head are accurately seeing the world, the situations we experience, our lives, our relationships—everything. As soon as you can recognize that you are not your thoughts, then you can begin to select which thoughts you are going to pay more attention to and which thoughts you can just discard.

By recognizing that you are not the thoughts in your head, you can start to detach from them and start living your life with purpose, on purpose, because you choose to have a good day today. And it will happen, of course, when you are trying to pay attention and remain objectively aware that something unexpected will happen and your brain will fall back into default mode, which is where Ego begins his interpretation. He takes over and interprets everything for you so you can figure out what to do next. As you begin to understand how to incorporate the recognition of Ego and what grounding feels like for you, please remember to be kind to yourself. If you are trying, that is amazing! Please give yourself a pat on the back when you recognize egoic thought and just say to yourself, "Wow, Ego is having a field day with that. But I'm back now." If you can get into meditating every day, that is a terrific way to practice peaceful recognition of egoic thought and the ways in which you can detach from it. We will get into meditation in much more detail later, but I want you to understand that you're on the right track as long as it is *you* that is deciding to do it. You are making the choices here, not Ego. When you catch the negative self-talk running, that's him! That's Ego, and that is your cue to pull yourself back down to the present moment by grounding yourself with facts based in reality. It's Monday, October 1, and there's nothing actually happening right now. Let's explore a little bit deeper what I mean when I talk about the role of Ego.

CHAPTER 3

Perhaps love is the process of my leading
you gently back to yourself.
—Antoine de Saint-Exupery, *The Little Prince*

The Process of Changing Our Lives: A Practical Guide

In this chapter, I would like to walk you through the steps to incorporate into your life in order to see positive changes. Every day, you can be a little more *you* just by understanding what to do and why you are doing it in the first place.

So, what do you do with your Ego now that you know he's been in the driver's seat this whole time? One exercise requires that you take some time to pay attention to the thoughts in your head and recognize which ones are egoic in nature and which ones might be purposeful or goal-directed thoughts. We have a responsibility to ourselves to do this work and make sure that our actions are based in reality and fact as opposed to egoic interpretations triggering emotional and behavioral reactions.

Now, try another exercise. Try saying to yourself something like, *I am going to get a glass of water.* That you did on purpose, and I call that a goal-directed thought. Did you notice any difference between that thought or that choice to get a glass of water and when Ego is talking? *Thoughts* are defined as "ideas or arrangements of ideas that are the result of the process of thinking." What I propose is that we can begin to wake up when we are in charge of our thinking, when we make decisions on purpose. We, us, you need to be in charge, not Ego.

There is a sharpness to the goal-directed thinking, just like when you think, purposefully, to yourself, *I'm going to get a glass of water.* When you say to yourself, *I am going to get a glass of water,* you are in charge. When Ego is in the driver's seat, it feels different. Those egoic thoughts are soft, smooth, and insidious how they creep in, and we don't even notice. We don't notice because we are so used to listening to him. *I don't need a glass of water. This book is dumb. Why would I get a glass of water? I actually have to pee. Oh, then I'll get a sandwich.*

Ego is talking all the time. It's the quiet voice that narrates everything we see. *It's sunny outside. That person is wearing shorts. I wonder if it's warm out? Today reminds me of that fun Halloween when I was a kid.*

And then, Ego takes you on a ride, playing mind movies for you where you are actually envisioning a memory. You find yourself, perhaps, lost in thought about that fun Halloween. But, while you are lost in thought, what's actually happening? You're not eight years old on Halloween. You are looking out the window. All of this started because you let Ego go about his business and you didn't even know what was happening. And why would you? This is normal. People's minds wander, right?

Of course, our minds wander from time to time, but I am encouraging a little more mindful attention of each moment so we can actually begin to live our lives consciously. There is so much happening in the world around us and there is a lot to get distracted with, but we do not need to allow it to affect us and affect our moods and behavior.

Thoughts trigger emotions. That's a clinical fact. If we are living our lives each day allowing egoic thoughts to trigger our emotions, then we are going to be living on a roller coaster of emotions, believing the whole time that they are valid. This is one origin of depression, anxiety, anger, hostility, and irritability; the list is endless. If we are not mindfully aware of which thoughts are triggering emotions, then we begin to react to the emotional state, believing this emotion is valid because the emotion matches up with the thought. And down the rabbit hole we fall, endlessly tumbling down, down, down until we find ourselves possibly engaging in constant arguments with our friends, loved ones, teachers, or bosses, or maybe we just hate ourselves for "being this way."

We are social beings, and if we leave Ego in charge, we are in big trouble. Left unchecked, we wander through our lives, past other people, with Ego interpreting their actions and behaviors. Ego is the thing that is determining that the person standing in front of you in line at the grocery store is a nice person because she is smiling and helping to bag her own groceries. As social beings, though, we may benefit more from remaining grounded in reality as we approach a social interaction as opposed to leaving Ego at such a time. Ego will tell you all about what is going to happen in that social encounter, if we let him, and it may not match up to the reality, thus, possibly, leading us into an unnecessary and emotionally complex situation.

Perhaps, Ego has also interpreted that the person whose cubical is next to yours at work is a mean person because he doesn't talk much and is very attractive. Maybe Ego tells you that this attractive person is not friendly because you are not attractive like he is, so you shouldn't put yourself out there just to be rejected. Ego's job is to keep you safe, after all. Ego may interpret his attractiveness for you by using a psychological defense mechanism to keep you from talking to him in order to keep you safe. And if you use your goal-directed thinking to choose to say hi to this person today, so you actually have something to base your opinion on, then maybe this person smiles and says hi back to you, thus changing your whole initial interpretation of him.

Ego is keeping us safe all the time, and he does so by having access to all of our psychological defenses. Not only does he have access to our psychological defenses, but he has also contributed to their use and design. Based on childhood experiences, Ego takes all of those times we felt uncomfortable, scolded, angry, sad, like we were bad people, selfish, or alienated and creates a defense specific for those times in our future that we may feel the same or similar so we do not have to suffer. Those feelings are not ideal, so Ego protects us from them. This is where behaviors come from.

Maybe a pretty person was mean to you in middle school. One, your Ego interpreted that person to be pretty. Two, Ego took that feeling of hurt or sadness because this person was mean to you and created a defense mechanism that translated to *All or most pretty people are mean*, so you avoid them as best you can in life; perhaps you even adopt a cynical view of attractive people and frequently talk badly about them because they must be mean, or maybe the only reason they got this far in life is because they used their looks to manipulate people.

We can change all of this. No matter how old you are or where you are in your life, you can change all of this. In order to live a fuller, more fulfilling, and tranquil life, you may need to change things.

I'm not talking about becoming some kind of delusional robot who only thinks positively all the time. That's ridiculous. Sometimes bad things happen, and we have to deal with them. We have to contend with the feelings that are triggered, our own behavioral reactions, and the actual situation and how to fix it. But we do not have to allow Ego to do all of that for us. If we do, like I said earlier, we're in trouble.

In order to change anything in the way that I am proposing, you do not *need* anything. You don't need a prescription from a doctor. You do not need to adhere to a specific diet. You just have to pay attention. Wake up and pay attention. Choose, right now, to stop living your life unconsciously and start paying attention to the voice in your head. Start watching your own thoughts. Practice becoming the objective observer of your own thoughts so as to remain in charge of which thoughts you need to pay attention to and which thoughts are merely egoic, and dismiss them.

One of the best ways to practice doing that is by using a technique called grounding. In that moment where you catch yourself caught up in egoic thought, you bring yourself back by saying to yourself, *Ooh, lost in egoic thought. Okay. Breathe in, breathe out, I'm back now. I am here. It is Friday, September 15.* Catch the egoic thought as you recognize you are lost. Don't analyze the egoic thoughts; that defeats the purpose, and you'll just find yourself aligned all over again with Ego and his interpretations of why this is happening. Catch it, and bring yourself back to exactly what you are doing in the moment you came back to present. Where are you? What are you doing? Reiterate for yourself what is actually happening right here and right now and then try to stay there for as long as you can.

In the beginning, as you are trying to make this a part of your everyday routine, it can feel like a mental tug-of-war. With all of the variations in your day-to-day, you may find yourself practicing grounding and detaching from egoic thought so frequently that the easier thing may be so tempting. The easier thing to do is nothing. The easier thing to do is exactly what you have been doing up to this point. Keep reading and keep practicing. I strongly recommend meditating, which I get into in much more detail later, but I will clue you into why it is so beneficial; when we are meditating, we are practicing Ego detachment. Very simply put, the practice of meditation is just dedicated time to clearing our minds by increasing our awareness and consciously detaching from egoic thoughts.

I am literally promising you positive results if you practice and make these tools part of your life. There is nothing bad that can come from this. I'm trying to spice it up a bit by telling you a little about me so you know that I'm a real human who totally sucked at life—or so my Ego told me for a very long time. These principles are here and yours for the taking. If we could all practice being a little more aware of what is actually happening and what is actually important and spend a little less time lost in egoic thought or trapped by egoic interpretation, the world might become a little better. We, collectively, might become a little better.

Regain control over your behavioral reactions toward yourself and others by practicing Ego detachment and grounding throughout your day, every day. Take responsibility for everything you are doing and saying because *you* are in charge of your life. You are in charge of you, not Ego and not egoic thoughts. Stop allowing those egoic thoughts to set the tone for your day, your week, and your life. Once you can make that choice, once you actually recognize the difference between the egoic thoughts and goal-directed thoughts, then you can begin to calmly proceed moving forward in your life.

There is more science behind this, and it is easily applied to everyday life. The science of psychology and the inner workings of our minds mixed with some basic mindfulness concepts and one simple technique is, perhaps, the recipe for curing this epidemic of unconscious, mindless living.

CHAPTER 4

Nothing in life is to be feared, it is only to be
understood. Now is the time to understand
more, so that we may fear less.
—Marie Curie

The Science behind the Change

I am not a scientist, per se, but I do have a clinical and
psychological background that has led to a comprehensive
understanding of how our brains function and why we
are, generally, the way we are. In my work as a clinician,
I have the opportunity to go deeper into specifics during
individual sessions, but here I will discuss the more basic
scientific aspects to ensure that you know how and why this
concept applies to everyone.

Psychological thought patterns and behavior patterns are
engrained in us from birth. We are all products of our
environment, to an extent, until we decide to take matters
into our own hands and become a product of our own
making. We are influenced by our parents' behaviors,

siblings' moods and temperaments, as well as our surrounding environment in general. All of this is how we make sense of the world around us. Ego interprets reality for us, and when we are young, we listen to him as our conscience, guiding us (hopefully) toward better choices. Or maybe we listen to Ego as that little angel on our shoulders reminding us, *You might not want to do that. Last time Mom got mad.* Or *remember you tripped and fell and that hurt. Maybe go the other way this time.* He can also play that little bad guy on our shoulders, encouraging us to do the bad thing for a more deeply rooted psychological purpose. Could he be encouraging us to do that bad thing for attention? A cry for help? Is Ego gently whispering to you that no one notices anyway so just do that bad thing to prove it to yourself that no one is paying attention? This is the reason, in short, why we have to wake up and start paying attention to our thoughts, to what Ego is telling us. If left unchecked, that negative line of thinking is going to get us into some serious trouble. The earlier in our lives that we can start to practice detaching from Ego, the more fulfilling and productive we will be. Let's get back to understanding how these thought patterns have been created.

We listen to Ego interpret for us, as children, all the time. He tells us what is happening in every situation, like when our parents are angry with us or disappointed and when they are happy and proud of us. And it is with those interpretations that we begin internalizing, or holding inside of us, our emotions with thoughts attached to them, as Ego has interpreted all of it. We begin developing how we feel about certain situations or certain people in our lives. We internalize it when we make an unconscious association with the situation or person. It is unconscious because it is Ego's interpretation. It is not conscious, or *on purpose* or because we decided it. It is Ego's best guess, and we often just go with it. As we internalize more of Ego's interpretations of events throughout our lives, we develop more defense mechanisms so Ego can keep us safe from those unpleasant situations. Our personalities are becoming solidified in those early years. Those initially created associations lead to our automatic thought patterns and automatic behavior patterns that shape our approach to everyday life. They are automatic because Ego set it all up and we just go with it. However, it is not permanent. We can reprogram certain aspects of how our minds process information now that we are in charge, and this is described in much more detail as we move toward understanding the science behind neuroplasticity.

As we get older, we tend to find ourselves in more challenging situations involving uncharted territory like relationships, jobs, marriage, mortgages, and maybe having children. And we continue through this uncharted territory attempting to manage the stress of the unknown the only way we know how, the way we learned since we were children. We listen to that voice in our head and all of its interpretations about everything. And we allow that voice in our head to determine the direction of our actions, our feelings, our jobs, our relationships, and our lives.

If we can detach from egoic thought, then we can truly make our lives exactly what we want them to be. But you might recall making excuses like, "It's just the way my mind works" or "I can't help the way I think." Lies! You can, and you will if you can dedicate a small amount of time and effort to learning how to regain control over your most powerful tool—your mind.

How many of us find ourselves anticipating a day off only to find that day riddled with anxiety, an inability to truly relax, and feelings of guilt or unworthiness? Why can't we just enjoy a day with no work and no deadlines—just us? The reason so many of us can relate to a scenario like this is because we are all human and we all have brains hardwired the same way. While we are all different in the ways in which we think and behave, we all have the same hardwiring that makes up our basic psychological functioning. We can relate because we have been there, to some degree or another. This is due to our overall collective programming that is universal to us all on an elemental level. The human brain can be studied and understood, in part, because the human brain works on electrical impulses that trigger specific responses. Scans of the human brain can illustrate when we are happy because areas of the brain literally light up with activity. Chemical reactions occur between neurotransmitters and hormones, which, in a way, feed Ego so he will keep interpreting why we are feeling happy. And the same thing happens when we are sad, nervous, or angry. Human behaviors can be studied in a similar manner. Our brains are built the same way, so they basically work the same way, yielding similar behavioral responses in similar situations.

So going back to why we can't relax, how is it that we feel we can only relax when we are busy or focused on doing some task? Probably because our minds don't "turn off" when we want to relax. Well, at least not until now. I will continue to demonstrate how the technique of detaching from egoic thoughts and grounding ourselves is helpful to practice throughout our days so we can quiet our minds and experience real peace and tranquility on a regular basis so we are not just left to deal with the chemical reactions in our brains and Ego's interpretation of it all.

Neuroplasticity and Rewiring Our Minds

In order for us to live our lives on purpose, or to wake up and live a conscious life, we have to identify the thought patterns that are working against us. Thought patterns lead to behavioral patterns, and they are all part of the neuroplasticity of our brains, the wiring or connections in our brains that have been formed over the course of our lives and all influenced by Ego's interpretations.

Neuroplasticity is defined as the brain's ability to rewire itself. To rewire our brains, we must be aware of what the existing connections are and what behaviors emerge from following them. Once we can uncover those connections, through traditional talk therapy or determined self-discovery, then we can begin to rewire our brains to exhibit fewer maladaptive responses to emotional triggers.

Whoa, Lindsey. Hold on a hot second. What does all that psychobabble mean? Good question.

Maladaptive responses to emotional triggers are the not-so-great ways we react when we are feeling anxious, sad, afraid, or mad. There's a reason for it, and it's a little different for all of us. There's a reason for everything, but I'll try to stay focused here and limit my explanations to thought content, getting back in control of our own minds, and waking up.

If Ego says, *That's not the way it works. You wasted your money on this stupid book. She makes it sound so simple, but if it were that simple, then you wouldn't feel this way. It's hopeless. I'll just figure it out on my own,* then chances are you're feeling pretty down. That is the maladaptive (not-so-good) response to an emotional trigger. The emotion that was triggered (activated or set off) was sadness or depression. Ego, in his attempts to keep you safe, just reinforced that another way couldn't possibly work, so don't waste your time trying. But that's his opinion. What's yours?

By looking closely at and recognizing egoic thought as it's happening, we can begin to rewire our thought patterns. If we are able to recognize egoic thinking and stop it—perhaps we imagine shoving it into a brightly colored balloon and letting go of the balloon—we begin to detach from Ego. We recognize that egoic interpretations are not useful and really serve no purpose, then we no longer feel the need to react emotionally. We don't need to get depressed because Ego just told us none of this would work. We shove that thought into a beautiful blue balloon and use goal-directed thinking to replace Ego's interpretation with *I am going to try this because I owe it to myself to feel better, and I did just recognize that voice was Ego, so maybe this Lindsey chick is on to something.*

The rewiring happens the instant that we recognize egoic thought, label it as such, and *choose to do something different.* Rewiring of the brain can happen, bit by bit. Imagine a lamp plugged into an outlet. That is how our brains are wired and how our thoughts are linked to our behaviors. Perhaps try this exercise: Write down your most common negative self-talk thoughts. Then write down your most negative or detrimental behaviors or habits. Compare the two for similarities and look for possible links. When we allow those negative and self-deprecating thoughts to become how we truly feel and how we believe others feel about us, we may adopt some negative behaviors as a direct result. For example, *I'm not good at math. I'm so stupid. It makes no sense to me. What's the point in trying?* Maybe the behavior you adopt is you stop trying to understand math. That was just one example, and I am sure that by making the lists, you will find connections to a few other negative behavioral or emotional responses. That negative thought narrated for you that you can't do it, and you went with it. Those negative behaviors only validate what we already believe to be true, and that was a result of aligning with the egoic thought in the first place. We also have emotional responses to negative thoughts, such as, *I am so awkward that everyone sees it. That has to be why I feel so alone. Who wants to be seen with the weird reject?* If that becomes a thought you truly identify with, your emotional reaction may be to feel depressed and so maybe you isolate yourself socially, which only validates that original thought further.

This creates a self-fulfilling prophecy, meaning that you incorrectly defined the situation, which then evokes or creates a new behavior that, in turn, makes the original, false conception come true. That thought added validation to what you already suspected, so it must be real. Right?

Wrong! It is a vicious cycle for many of us, and it needs to stop. Even further, it is our egoic interpretation that we are good or bad in general based on Mom or Dad's facial expression, tone of voice, or words said. For example, perhaps you were five years old, playing with your sister and your stuffed animals, when Mom came into the room with a harsh, angry look on her face. Maybe you didn't really notice at first and you continued playing. But then she walked back into the room, turned her back to you, and shouted, "You never listen to me, and I'm sick and tired of it!" This is where Ego interprets for you that she is mad at you because you didn't clean up the room like she had asked you to. But, in real life, she had turned her back to you because she was actually yelling at your father, and, in reality, she had no problem with you or what you were doing. But Ego did what he does best, and he gave you something to internalize based on his assumptions about what you witnessed. It is important to note here that when we are young, we are not yet able to fully comprehend anything outside of ourselves. Children are considered egocentric because they can only think about themselves and have not yet developed the ability to consider someone else's feelings. They are egocentric, or *ego centered,* because they blindly listen to Ego doing what he is psychologically programmed to do— interpret the situation or tell them what is happening. So children may always interpret a situation, like the one just described, as all about them even when it had nothing to do with them.

It is in this way that we find ourselves, in our young adult and adult lives, questioning ourselves when we are self-conscious or when we are positive that we can't do something. It is rooted in our egoic interpretations of things from our past. Conversely, these can also be reinforced if in fact your mother or father told you that you were incapable in some way or another. In those situations, Ego absorbs it and owns it forever, creating defense mechanisms to protect you from feeling that way but also narrating for you and reinforcing to you that you are not capable.

Thought always triggers emotion, so when we have a thought, it automatically leads to our feeling a certain way, which leads Ego to interpret for us and protect us by arming us with psychological defenses. *Sally just looked at me sideways (thought) and now I feel rejected(feeling), so I'm going to ignore her (defense).* All of this is a behavior pattern. It's a behavior pattern because it's what we do to protect ourselves from feeling rejected again. Maybe we get defensive anytime anyone looks at us sideways. Now, go back to the lamp plugged into an outlet. That is our brain's connection; when someone looks at us sideways, we always ignore them because we are "plugged into" one outlet. Now imagine if plugging that lamp into a different outlet would make the light from the lamp brighter. By recognizing the connections between thought and feeling and feeling to behavior, we are rewiring our brains and changing our behavior, thus leading to an improved quality of life and more rational, goal-directed thinking. Perhaps this will result in a feeling of stability and oneness as opposed to that original feeling of alienation and isolation. The rewiring happens when we choose to plug our lamps into a different, more functional, outlet. The first step is awareness. You have to notice it if you are going to change any of it. And, boy, is it tough. Rewiring the mind is no easy task. The hardest part is going to be catching yourself reacting the way you used to, stopping, and making yourself react differently. If you can catch it, that moment when you are reacting, and you are successful in reacting in a more productive way, then you just need to remain aware of those moments and repeat the process. If you can remain consistent, then you will quickly establish new neural pathways that will serve as your new and improved thought and behavioral patterns.

Many of us have some degree of a daily routine. And while our daily routines may feel monotonous and boring, there are slight variations in our days every day, many of which go unnoticed. Think about it. You get up in the morning after hopefully getting a decent night's sleep. You shower, but maybe this morning you tripped over your daughter's stuffed animal while you were putting your pants on only to fall on your face and it wasn't even seven o'clock. So, then you were frustrated that your daughter had left her things all over the house, so you tried talking to her about the importance of organization. But she's five and doesn't really care for what you're trying to talk to her about, so she is not paying attention. You, perhaps, become more frustrated and just try to focus on packing her lunch for school. Fast forward to the moment you dropped your daughter off at school and now you have to get yourself to work. You had a frustrating morning, and now you just want to get to work. But you get stuck behind a school bus, and this makes you feel as though you are never going to get to work. Frustrated beyond belief, you cut down a side street and get pulled over going fifty miles per hour in a twenty-five miles per hour residential area. In New Jersey, that will automatically result in points on your license (not that I would know), and it will absolutely require you to go to court and pay a pretty hefty fine (again, not that I have any personal experience with speeding).

That was just a hypothetical portion of one morning and some of the variations that one can experience. While we may feel our lives are somewhat boring and too repetitive, we are unaware—unconscious, if you will—of all the details that are shaping our feelings, our moods, and our behaviors. Take that scenario, for example. How many of you can relate to something similar in your own morning routine? And how many of you have ever been aware of the thoughts that are narrating your mornings for you? If we are not aware of the thoughts, then we just allow them to trigger emotions, shape our moods, and season our behavioral reactions. In that scenario, you first became frustrated because you tripped and fell. If you had been able to watch the thoughts leading up to tripping and falling, perhaps you could have been slightly more aware of your surroundings and could have avoided falling in the first place. But instead, you were preoccupied with *thoughts* of your daughter's haphazard toy storage, which led to the behavior of trying to address the "problem," as you see it.

With all of these variations in our daily routines, it can be pretty challenging to practice mindful awareness in order to rewire our brains. It may feel like constant work. Who has time for that?

Are you serious? No, really—if you've had that thought, *Who has time for all of this? I have real work to do and kids to take care of and money to manage,* you owe it to yourself to keep reading and to dedicate time and energy to these practices. Seriously, you don't have time to take responsibility for the thoughts in your own mind? If you don't have time for that, then I feel sorry for you, living life so unconsciously that you don't even know what you don't know. You are so busy and so frazzled that you believe that you have no choice but to be a victim in your own life. Stop all of those thoughts. Breathe. Come back to right here, right now, in this moment. Stop all of these racing thoughts and breathe. This is all there is, right now, right here. You're sitting and reading. That's it.

We've recognized the voices in our heads—which one is truly us and which one is Ego. We've also learned about the science behind our behavioral patterns and how to change them, by rewiring our brains. This is already a lot of work to do! Literally, I am talking about changing the way you live each day, and it is a challenge. This is not easy work, which is why I suggest finding a good, mindful, therapist to go with you on this journey. A lot of people out there have their own interpretation of why we are the way we are, and they too have a lot of science to support it. And that's fine. I stumbled upon this through my own personal journey, and I introduced small pieces to some of my clients in outpatient therapy. When they started applying it to their lives, their lives started improving. Things started improving because they started taking charge of their interpretations of their own lives. Did they still face challenges? Of course. Do I still wrestle with egoic thoughts at times? Of course. I'm not a robot. You are not a robot. We are human beings with emotions. I am just trying to help people get in control of their emotions so they can remain human beings with emotions as opposed to emotions with human beings. Who's in charge? I hope it's you. If you have ever struggled with depression, anxiety, anger, and so on, you can take control and find peace. It takes time, dedication, and practice, but over time, it will become your second nature. It can become as effortless as blinking. This is truly the science behind psychological functioning in a form that can be used by everyone. We are all human. We all have brains, and each of our brains is hardwired to function with Ego narrating the world around us in order to keep us safe. Ego is narrating for every single person on the planet, *unless* they have practiced mindful attention to those thoughts, disconnected from them, and practiced remaining present in the moment, every moment. Those are basic, psychological facts. The endless combinations of life circumstances make us who we are—unique and different based on genetics, predispositions, family circumstances, and so on. Ego should not be in charge, but he is for most people and they don't even know it. And that is okay. But do you want to remain so unconscious, so oblivious to reality that you may never wake up?

I would like to focus my efforts on those who want to live their lives with purpose, on purpose, the people who want to have a say in their own lives and how they view all of the experiences that shape them, and the people who choose happiness. It's those people who, I know, have known fear, sadness, loss, and trauma. Those are the people who deserve to wake up and live the life they were meant to live. For anyone who has suffered, you deserve to take your life back. Stop playing the victim and take back your life. I'm giving you the map. Take it. Follow it. And you will see for yourself.

CHAPTER 5

If we hope to go anywhere or develop ourselves
in any way, we can only step from where we
are standing. If we don't really know where we
are standing … we may only go in circles.
—Jon Kabat-Zinn, *Wherever You Go, There You
Are: Mindfulness Meditation in Everyday Life*

Mindfulness, Meditation, and Spirituality

We've learned about Ego, the process of grounding, and
some of the science behind why and how all of this works.
Now it's time to expand our minds in order to feel fulfilled
and at peace in every moment of every day.

How can we take all the Ego stuff about our thoughts and all
of the science behind neuroplasticity and behavior patterns
and actually improve our lives? *Geez, Lindsey. What are you
writing here? This is like the owner's manual for my brain.*
I know, Ego, thank you for that interpretation. Seriously,
though, we can slow things down and get back in control
of ourselves every moment of every day. Learning how to

become mindful is a large component to slowing things down and improving our daily lives. Adopting a mindful lifestyle will move us toward calmer, more rewarding lives, no matter who we are or what our circumstances are.

Lots of people talk about mindfulness, but lots of people also differ in their interpretations of what mindfulness is and is not. I say mindfulness is awareness. I also say mindfulness is being firmly planted in the present moment, at every moment. If we can quiet the Ego and practice being present in the moment, then we can react appropriately to every moment without egoic interpretations getting in the way and telling us how we should feel.

Sit still, right now. Breathe in and breathe out. Pay attention to whatever else is in your head. Now imagine shoving all of that into a bunch of balloons and letting them go. Focus on your breathing again. Pay attention only to breathing. This is mindfulness. Mindfulness is awareness, awareness of right here and right now. Inhale. Exhale. You are kind of meditating.

Meditating

Meditation has several misinterpretations. It is actually much simpler than you think. When I have talked about meditation, I have encountered many who think they are supposed to think nothing, but that's close to impossible. In reality, it is the practice of paying attention to the present moment, and an easy way to try it is to pay close attention to breathing in and breathing out—inhaling and exhaling.

Over and over again, it quiets the mind (and the Ego) if you are able to get to a point where you are making yourself concentrate (goal-directed) on only breathing in and breathing out. Sometimes I attach numbers to it as I go. Breathing in, breathing out, one; breathing in, breathing out, two; and so on. Ego has no place here, and by slowing things down in this manner, your physical body can begin to slow down as well. Your heart rate decreases, as does your blood pressure. You can begin to feel at peace.

That is until Ego tries to slip in there and play a mind movie for you. Ego plays these mind movies frequently because this is what we have allowed him to do for our entire lives. We do nothing and just let Ego drive. The practice of mindfulness includes meditation just as a healthy lifestyle includes eating vegetables or going to the gym. The practice of meditation can be thought of as the mind's gym. The goal here is to quiet those egoic thoughts, focus on right here, right now, and be able to generalize this practice so we can draw from this calm place when we are faced with daily struggles.

While you were practicing meditation, Ego may have seen an opportunity to give you something to worry about that required his interpretation so he could stay employed and keep you safe from potential danger. Ego can be useful in a real crisis, but he has many of us living in a constant state of crisis, which is unnecessary. Meditating is the practice of detaching from that constant state of crisis.

In meditation, we consciously choose to focus our thoughts and attention on one thing. I feel that, in beginning to practice meditation, focusing on breathing in and breathing out can be most helpful in staying focused. I also recommend a quiet space. It doesn't have to be soundproof, but especially when starting your practice, minimal distractions are helpful to remaining focused on the breath. The act of meditating can and will quiet your egoic mind because you are using your goal-directing thinking in your choice to sit down and breathe in order to quiet your mind. Personally, I have a meditation cushion on the floor in a corner of my home office, and it is behind a beautiful folding screen. So even when someone else is home, I still feel like I have my space to sit and concentrate my mind even if someone needs to come into the room to get a stamp for an envelope. I do recommend sitting as opposed to lying down for a very simple reason: you will fall asleep! This practice in relaxation is so calming that as soon as our egoic mind is quiet, we are at peace completely. Falling asleep is probably the most common thing to happen to all of us when we begin.

So, let's get into the details. If you want to practice meditation, simply find a quiet space with minimal distractions, and sit cross-legged while maintaining a straight back, but not to the point of causing tension. Allow your arms to rest on your lap with your palms facing up where they are comfortable. Close your eyes, focusing them on the point between your eyebrows, and breathe. While breathing in and breathing out, I also attach numbers to help keep Ego out. For example, "Breathing in, breathing out, one; breathing in, breathing out, two," and so on. While only focusing on your breathing, try to count as high as you need to until you feel your mind become still and quiet. When you get there, keep breathing normally. I may simply affirm to myself something like, "Quiet mind, calm heart," while I make a conscious effort to increase my positive energy with gratitude. While breathing, focusing my eyes at the point between the eyebrows, I consciously bring into my awareness thoughts of what I am most grateful for today. I use a timer to keep me focused also. There are many free apps for your phone that will all work the same way. I use the Insight Timer, and I set it for however long I have to meditate—ten minutes, twenty minutes, an hour. I use some simple background noise also so that if the floor creaks or my dog barks, I am not torn completely from my meditation, and a simple bell sounds when I have reached my allotted time limit. When I hear that my time is up, I make sure that I am aware of this state of serenity and peace. I take a few deeper breaths while bringing my hands together to the center of my chest, bow my head, and thank the universe for showing me this peace by saying to myself, *Namaste*.

The more frequently we practice meditating, the more frequently we may find ourselves existing in each and every moment so much more than before. Especially after a meditation practice where you spent any amount of time in that serene tranquility without Ego, make the conscious effort to keep Ego out. Reflect back on that feeling of complete peace and allow that to become the new normal in your daily routine. Slow down, shrink the scope of life's troubles, and just breathe. Focus your energy on what you actually have control over. You have no control over other people, so why spend so much time allowing Ego to narrate what *they* mean or what *they're* thinking? Who cares? What are *you* thinking? You can control what you are thinking as long as you can recognize the difference between egoic thought and goal-directed thinking. It is there in that moment that you choose goal-directed thinking that you take away some of Ego's power over your mind.

Meditation is the practice that allows you to know the difference between how you have allowed you mind to run amok and how it feels to be mentally at peace. It is healthy, it is free, and the enormous amount of psychological and medical benefits of meditating are at your fingertips. Meditation is the practice, but you have to know why you are doing it and what you will get out of it.

By making the effort to meditate daily, even just for fifteen minutes, you are strengthening your mind just as you go to the gym to strengthen your muscles. You are training your mind to let go of egoic thoughts and remain present and grounded in this moment. This method of brain training will come in handy the next time life throws you a curveball, which it frequently does when you least expect it. You will be jarred, perhaps, but not derailed because you will be able to replace Ego's interpretation of the events with simpler, goal-directed thinking that relates to this moment and what you actually have control over. You will be able to take an objective stance in your own life when you learn how to detach from egoic thoughts. You will be able to take a step back and make a rational decision that is not directed by an egoic and emotional reaction.

For example, imagine that your boss calls you into her office and, after making small talk, begins to critique your performance as well as your wardrobe. As this tension mounts, you find your egoic mind wandering into defensive tactics: *What is she talking about? How could she just give me a compliment about my impeccable work ethics last week but now say I'm terrible and messing everything up? Am I really that bad? Maybe I have been slacking lately.* You perhaps find yourself retreating inward because it doesn't feel nice to be critiqued, especially when you are taken off guard. This is Ego protecting you by pushing the actual *you* down so he can step in and put up a force field to protect you from this attack. While this is a very unfortunate curveball, you have been practicing meditation and mindful techniques to help in a situation like this. While you are "under attack," you can *choose* to recognize what you know for a fact (goal-directed thinking): you know that you are performing well and that it shows in your numbers. You know that you have been consistent in your performance and have not been slacking lately. You can recognize that this came out of left field and your boss must be having a rough day, week, month, or whatever. Life threw you a curveball, and you can remain present in this moment—even though you really just want to run away or adamantly defend yourself—and you, the actual *you,* can narrate this for yourself with the facts. Then your goal-directed thinking can take over while Ego goes to get a snack. Now the real you is in the driver's seat, and you can find some relief from all of those terrifying emotions that Ego was protecting you from. Replace those egoic thoughts with, *It's Friday, September 29, and I'm being verbally attacked by my boss. I know what I am doing, and it is a real shame that she thinks I am not doing a good job. I do not have to feel unworthy or completely inept because I know my job and I know I take it seriously. I respect myself, and I will let her go on her rant and decide a little later what is in my power to do about this.*

It is because of your meditation practice that you may have been able to talk yourself down while being attacked by your boss. Maybe it doesn't go that smoothly, but at least you were able to get *you* in the driver's seat so Ego didn't have a complete overreaction by yelling back at your boss or getting *you* so worked up that *you* storm out of her office and really put your job in jeopardy.

By meditating somewhat regularly, you can calm those once volatile emotions. Meditation can help to reinforce the neural pathway in your brain that is responsible for the behavioral reaction to those emotions, and you can spend more time in a tranquil state rather than on a volatile, emotional roller coaster.

I am going right back to the science and neuroplasticity. All of this is real. All of this is proven, in pieces, in science. We can rewire our brains. We can change our automatic thought patterns and our automatic behavioral patterns.

By practicing meditation as frequently as you can, you create a point of reference for your brain, and this will make the rewiring part much easier. The point of reference is the peace and serenity that you begin to feel as you get better at detaching from egoic thoughts. Once you do it, you will have rewired your brain to understand what you mean when you catch yourself in egoic thought and detach from it. Once you know what serenity feels like, you will be able to get back there. Our brains love patterns, and this is a pattern you will also love to repeat.

The more we meditate and the more we take responsibility for our thoughts and behaviors, the more we will also find ourselves conscious and aware of the beauty in each and every moment.

By practicing a mindful approach to each day, I only suggest gentle reminders to come back to the present every time we notice we are aligned with, or lost in, egoic thought. Has anyone ever told you that thinking too much is a bad thing? Well, if they have, they were right. If no one ever told you that, I just did. It's a thing, and it's true. Thinking too much is usually egoic thinking because Ego is interpreting the situation for you. Thinking too much can happen when we are stressed or depressed or overanxious or in so many situations. Thinking too much might sound like, *I hope my boss isn't disappointed in my performance this quarter. I should probably say I'm sorry. No, if I say I'm sorry then my boss is going to think I'm weird, but maybe I should wait until we have my review and then say I'm sorry and that will show that I was prepared and I am being proactive and that's a good thing. I'll have to make sure I dress well for that meeting, and I'll start drafting my own performance improvement plan so that my boss will be pleased she doesn't have to do it.*

That was horrible! It was exhausting to follow that. Thinking too much and being lost in thought are synonymous, in my opinion, and they are bad. All of that is Ego. You will not *think* your way out of a situation. I understand the tendency to plan in order to not be caught off guard, but that is not working in the way you may have hoped. That was incessant chatter that would only lead to intense anxiety if left unchecked. That was Ego telling you that your boss is not going to be happy with your performance. Did your boss tell you that she was unhappy with your performance? No? Then what are you doing? Are you psychic? Then stop acting like you know what your boss is thinking.

We have to be in charge of our minds, and we have a responsibility to ourselves to stop the negative self-talk; the negative and sometimes catastrophic mind movies; and the ruminating or obsessively thinking about sad, scary, or stressful things. All of that is Ego, not you. We stop this by grounding ourselves and attempting to gain perspective. When we catch our egoic mind running away with itself, we have to catch it and pull it back down to planet Earth, to the right here and right now. Right here, in this moment, what do you have to do? What is actually happening? Maybe nothing at all, but you need to remind yourself of that because Ego would have you watch those frightening mind movies all day, where you are visualizing all of the terrible things that could happen while losing time in your life. Instead, catch Ego, detach from those pointless and worrisome thoughts by grounding yourself, and reaffirm for yourself what is actually happening in this moment. If you recognize that Ego seems to come back swiftly after you have grounded yourself, just take a breath and tell yourself that it is all right and Ego is just having a good time. Ground yourself again, and then it's okay to do an activity: walk the dog, fold the laundry, play a video game. As long as you are grounded in awareness and detached from egoic thought, it is perfectly fine to do an activity. It is only detrimental when you are not grounded in awareness and you are trying to avoid those egoic thoughts. When we try to hide from Ego, we are actually making him more powerful.

When we can practice mindfulness, we can be present in the moment and react to what is actually happening. Suppose in that horribly exhausting chunk of time that you'll never get back, while you were lost in thought about your boss and your performance improvement plan, you were at your daughter's first soccer game. You just lost all of that precious time. You were lost in thought, completely aligned with Ego while he was telling you what you need to worry about, and you missed your five-year-old daughter make her first goal. Maybe you only snapped out of it when you heard the parents around you cheering, and then you realized what happened, what you missed, only to give Ego some fresh material to torture you with. Because if you are not practicing mindfulness in that scenario, Ego will have a field day, immediately interpreting how bad a parent you are because you weren't paying attention. Or perhaps Ego is in a particularly foul mood and decides to mention that *your job is what pays for her to play soccer, so you need to worry about this and plan for this and maybe you would be better off meeting them at home so you can plan how you are going to advocate for your position.* Maybe you do that, and your innocent little five-year-old watches you leave her first game, and there you go giving her little ego something to have a field day with when she is in therapy in ten years.

In that moment, why couldn't you use some of the techniques I'm offering? In that moment, where you catch yourself lost in egoic thought, bring yourself back to present as the crowd cheers for your little athlete. Then, take a deep breath and replace the egoic thought with goal-directed thoughts such as, *Whoa, I missed that. I am back, and I am going to remain here for her. I am right here, right now, and this is what matters in this moment.*

Mindfulness is the ability to remain firmly planted in the reality of each moment as it comes. This practice can be challenging at first, but rather quickly it can become the new way you navigate your life. With each time you recognize that you were lost in egoic thought, bring yourself right back to right here and right now and start narrating your reality in a goal-directed way. There are a few specific ways to practice remaining mindful, one of which is letting go of a cynical or skeptical perspective and opening to an expansive and truly energizing way to live life. Open yourself up to a deeper understanding of yourself and what you are meant to do in your life. We know now that we are not meant to live unconsciously attached to our egoic thoughts but, rather, aware, more objective, detached from Ego so that we can reconnect with our souls through meditating regularly and developing a compassionate and spiritual awareness of the souls we encounter through this lifetime.

Spirituality

Perhaps, once we can get through the layers of Ego attachment, we can begin to understand that we are not our bodies inasmuch as we are not our thoughts. We are beautiful souls who rely on our bodies to fulfill our true purposes in this lifetime. To believe that we are our bodies, is another aspect of Ego attachment. This is perhaps where some may fall into an egotistical or self-absorbed way of living because the body and everything on the outside is held in the highest regard in our society. To be spiritual, I believe, is to reconnect with our souls in order to deeply feel and know our true purpose that is shrouded by Ego and the attachments that Ego will have us believe define us.

Up to this point, we have begun to understand what that voice in our heads actually is and why Ego is a part of our brains. From there, we explored aspects of Ego detachment and why this is so important, especially in attempting to combat any form of intense emotional reactions. Then we learned a bit about the science of neuroplasticity and how that involves Ego and, conversely, how we can use it to our advantage in detaching from Ego. As I bring us full circle, I introduced my perception of mindfulness and meditation, and here we can go deeper into the concept of spirituality.

This is something else that is much more openly discussed, and it goes hand in hand with a mindful approach to every day. Everyone is on his or her own journey in life, but for those of us who have found ourselves working on ourselves in an attempt to improve our lives, we may also find our way toward understanding the spiritual perspective.

I view spirituality as our individual understanding of our purpose and our deeper connection with the divine source of all of life. Some call it God and some call it Spirit, but

I don't want to get hung up on names. It's that something that gives us each our own individual life path, the thing that we search for—purpose and direction. It was a long journey for me to find my understanding of spirituality, and I would never go back to the unconscious life I was living. I am awake now, more often than not, and I meditate as much as I can so that I can feel connected to that divine source.

This is really where the practice of meditation comes into play if we are working on managing our emotions and our lives in general. By practicing recognizing egoic thoughts; detaching from them, perhaps through meditation; and then recognizing that there is so much more beyond this life and our assumed existential beginning and end, we can find our way to a deeper understanding of connectedness. It will go beyond an understanding, perhaps—an intuition, a knowing.

I am only offering a little of my own belief. All of these techniques can be applied regardless of whether or not you feel any amount of spirituality or interconnectedness. Just having a feeling that our true purpose is to live our lives and wake up to fully actualize and realize that we are more is sufficient. And we have an obligation to remember our purpose and remember that we are already connected to this divine source, and we can see through all of those little variations of every day—the flat tire, the bad weather, the tantrum-throwing children, the bills, the frustrations with work, and so on. We can take solace in knowing that, beyond all of those things, we are connected and we can move beyond the frustrations we face every day.

This is my view on being spiritual. I feel guided by life unfolding before me, and I know, deeply in my soul, that it's all happening for a reason. And that brings me peace, deep inner peace—when I can remember, that is. It can be incredibly difficult to remain focused and centered and grounded through our lives. But this is where the practice of ego detachment comes in. The more we practice detaching from egoic thought and the more we can take an objective perspective and maintain objective awareness, the easier life becomes. The detachment from Ego leads to an increased ability to manage our emotions and regulate ourselves. And maybe, for some, we find our way to spirituality and the world becomes that much more beautiful and every day becomes that much more exciting.

Why should we allow ourselves to get so bogged down by thoughts and worries and fears when we can learn how to detach from them and sort them appropriately to be free from them and connect with our higher purpose? We can learn how to connect with that divine source that never wanted us to suffer in the first place. We can live the life that we were always supposed to live, that life where we know we are all connected because we all come from the same source. And the spiritual source gives us all the opportunity to find our way back to a deeper understanding of the direction we need to go, the way back to the Source. Let's learn how to detach from Ego and manage our emotional reactions that Ego has had at his disposal for our entire lives so that we can truly regain our freedom to live and stop judging others. Everyone is on his or her own path. It is not anyone's job to tell anyone else which way the right way is. That is what spirituality, I believe, suggests—connectedness and peace from within.

Everything Happens for a Reason

I am a big believer in the concept that everything in our lives happens for a reason. If we practice mindful awareness in our everyday lives, then we can actually receive what life is offering us, whether that be a lesson through tragedy or unpleasant circumstance or a gift just for being aware enough to receive it.

If we learn to surrender to the flow of our individual lives and we maintain a mindful state of awareness to the here and now, then we can reap the benefits of living this beautiful life. Yes, it is possible even through the fog of depression or a seemingly relentless anxiety disorder to see the beauty in every day and to find happiness in every day.

And yes, again, it is incredibly difficult to do. Why? Well, back in the science portion of the book, I described the neuroplasticity of our brain's structure. And I touched on the concept that it is incredibly difficult at first to adopt these new ways of thinking because most of our minds are hardwired to do the opposite. Many of us are being driven by egoic impulse that feels completely justified in its rationalization. It *feels* like it makes sense to us why we are feeling the way we are and why we are then reacting in the way that we are. It seems like everything matches up.

But if everything happens for a reason, then why do you feel the heartache or stress or feeling of being overwhelmed? Because you didn't know it could be any other way. Something happens and Ego interprets what happened and kind of narrates it back to you, as if your own eyes and ears weren't enough. Ego tells you what it actually meant in the context of your own experiences, which then triggers an emotional response. Based on what, though? Based solely on Ego. But you don't know that, so you begin to feel emotional about whatever just happened and then you react, thanks to a good ol' nudge from Ego since he is telling you that you don't deserve to be treated in that way or you should stand up for yourself.

We all have our own cognitive maps, or cognitive schematics, and they are built by our experiences and how Ego interprets them for us. Those experiences are then stored, and they become our frame of reference for future experiences. For example, you know that I was depressed early in my life. My ego used that as my primary cognitive map for many years. This translated to a crippling depression and anxiety disorder that I battled for years because the internal dialogue was constantly self-deprecating. *Your boss clearly sees that you're a complete idiot and that you don't know half of what you should know for a position like this. You know you're faking and you don't really know what you're doing. You know you're not good enough. And, you know what? Everyone else sees it too. He knows you're a mess and it's only a matter of time before everyone gets sick of it just like all the others did and you'll be out on your ass again looking like the complete idiot that you are. You should just pretend. Keep pretending because otherwise they'll all see it and they'll all know. They don't need to know. Put on a mask. Keep pretending. That's the only way you'll make it. Keep your head down and stay quiet. You're not funny either, so stop being annoying to everyone around you because you think you're funny.*

I could go on and on describing the terrible things my ego has said to me in the past, but I won't because my point is that, despite carrying that funky broken record around in my mind for years, I offer to you now a solid approach to taming the voice in your head and taking charge of your own life. Because *everything happens for a reason!*

If I had never been born into the family that I have under the circumstances into which I was born, at the time in our society's growth and development, in the exact location in New Jersey that I was born, then I would not be who I am today and I would not have stumbled onto this path that I am currently on, having *learned* from *all* of my mistakes, which I like to think I have, and still be open to new lessons from past transgressions. If everything didn't happen exactly as it did, then I wouldn't be exactly who I am today. I am still a person who is working on herself. I don't think this work ever stops. It might just get a little easier after a while of really dedicating time and effort to it.

Everything happens for a reason, if we can only maintain our mindful awareness in order to actually receive the lesson or the gift. It all doesn't need to be so tragic. It's not that serious, and it is always and will always remain a matter of perspective on your part. If you can practice objectively observing your thoughts, taking steps to recognize egoic thoughts versus goal-directed thoughts while remaining present in this moment with the help of practicing meditating, then you'll get there too.

I know it sounds like too much—unmanageable even. Maybe you're too busy to do that work on top of everything else you're trying to manage. *Geez, Lindsey. I have a life, you know, and this would take me all day.* It will not. Ego is telling you, very naturally, that it is too much and it probably wouldn't work anyway. Of course he is. He doesn't want you to take the reins. What would he do with all his spare time if you took control over what is in your head?

All of those who are living life unconsciously are basically on autopilot with Ego behind the wheel of their lives. But if you can stop for a moment and recognize that this is all real and you have all you need to get started right now, then you're halfway there already. Get out of your own way, stop for a moment, and breathe. Take a deep breath in and say to yourself, "Inhale." On the breath out, say, "Exhale." Do this a few times and then pay attention to what happens next. Was that Ego? *What time is it? You don't have all day to sit here and breathe. Who's looking at you? Open your eyes and see who sees what you're doing. You should grab lunch.*

Yup. That was him all right. But when did you catch him? At the end? Earlier? Good. You caught Ego, and for that, I congratulate you. This is the practice. Slow your mind down, breathe, and catch Ego, and then you can begin to learn the difference between the egoic thinking that has ruled your life up to this point. And then you can more clearly begin to see goal-directed thinking and the times when *you* are actually in control of your own life.

This practice is a process that requires dedication. After practicing consistently every day, catching the egoic thoughts and detaching from them quickly by grounding yourself with facts of where you are or the date, then you free up a lot more time to be present with a quieter mind than you had before. And with that quiet mind comes peace and tranquility. Perhaps it will be fleeting at first, but continue to practice and the periods of peace and tranquility will become numerous and eventually permeate your soul. You will have found the ability to receive those beautiful gifts life is offering you on a regular basis, and you'll learn the lessons life is offering with essentially no more suffering. Life doesn't want us to suffer. Life isn't trying to punish you or me or anyone else. Life is trying to encourage all of us to wake up by giving us the tough stuff. Through the toughest trials, do you give up or forge onward? Do you forge onward with your eyes closed because it's easier that way? I hope not because you'll just end up tripping and falling all over again. If we don't accept the lesson that life is offering us by placing us in a tough situation, then we will just encounter it time and time again until we can learn and truly become aware of what's happening. It is through this process that we can move forward and the vicious cycle will end.

The work never stops. It just becomes more natural over time. The results you see in yourself and in your life are purely dependent on the amount of effort you put in. Some may find relief in a matter of weeks, while others may struggle with Ego a bit more. And that's okay. Any mindful practice does not need critiquing. Just the fact that you are trying means you are going to get there, and that's great.

There was a point in my life when, I can now see, I was completely lost. I was more unconscious than I can even believe. How did I function? How did I get myself into and out of some pretty dangerous situations? I feel like this is a perfect place to go a bit deeper into the concept that everything in life happens for a reason.

I can recall one such reckless decision I made when I was a teenager. I had just gotten grounded for something, but I wanted to go visit my boyfriend, who lived about thirty minutes away from me at the time. I decided to blindly call a cab company. I may have had a beeper back then, but that would have been no help if I had found myself in trouble. I did what I wanted to do—so impulsive.

Well, the cab showed up, and the driver was a younger man, maybe in his thirties. Yeah, I thought, *What am I doing?* But it was too late to turn back now, I thought. I initially went to get in the back seat when the man suggested I sit up front with him. *Yeah, totally not freaking out.*

To my thankful surprise, he was spiritually enlightened. I can only be clear on this now because, as I mentioned before, this was a period of my life when I was completely unconscious and completely unaware of anything beyond my own egoic interpretations of my world. But that is all the more reason to include it right here in this portion of the book. Everything happens for a reason, and I was picked up by a spiritually enlightened young man who spoke to me about the quest toward enlightenment when I, myself, was the farthest thing from enlightened for a reason. Because in this moment, I would finally be able to use it, to benefit from his knowledge, and to share the message.

This young man drove me to my destination on a Friday night in July 1999. I cannot recall in any detail what we spoke about or how we got to talking, but I vividly remember his strongly recommending that I read *The Celestine Prophecy* by James Redfield. I vividly remember that book, but I cannot recall why.

I never read the book. I was unconscious, remember? I thanked him for his time, for the great conversation, and for not being crazy. He left me with very kind words of encouragement, and it all became an instant memory. I was ego-driven, I was at my boyfriend's house, and I was more focused on what I could do to make sure that I was the prettiest version of myself while we were together so he'd continue to like me. That was my biggest focus back then—*present the best version of yourself, Lindsey; otherwise, they'll walk away.* And this is where the neuroplasticity comes into play again. Our brains love patterns, and when we are living unconscious lives, we don't even realize that we are subconsciously recreating the patterns that we find so troubling. If I had never woken up, I'd find myself subconsciously trying to destroy everything I've built in my life because my original pattern was to be miserable and lonely, never feeling good enough for anyone, especially myself. Even today, I catch myself making those same mistakes, leading me back to a dark place that feels as familiar as it does isolating. If we can bring our awareness into the present moment more often, we can recognize what we are doing, detach from Ego, and make a different choice. We can change it if we are awake and aware.

I reflect back on it now because, for no particular reason, I have been feeling aimless recently. I stumbled upon the idea that it may be in part due to my not reading a book currently. I am usually reading something spiritual these days. That memory resurfaced, and it resurfaced strongly! I ordered a book online because I felt a strong feeling that this would be one I would reference and refer to others. I began to read a sample, and I cannot describe to you the eerie yet fabulous sensation I felt as it all opened with the coming of a psychological transformation on the planet in my lifetime. In so many words, the sample was saying, *Everything in life happens for a reason.*

What that little sample did not include, however, was any instructions on how to achieve the transformation. Instead, it hinted at some things that would just randomly happen to some select few individuals who were able to achieve some level of awareness of things beyond themselves and their egoic interpretations of their lives. All of this led me to feel strongly that this message of managing our thoughts and taking back control of our lives needs to be out in the world. Perhaps the eeriest part of it all is that there are and have been books and movies about this topic for decades! There have been whispers about this idea for a very long time, but maybe we have come to a place in our lives, collectively, that allows for this transformation to occur. More of us have reached an impasse in our lives, and maybe we are ready to wake up now. More of us have struggled with anxiety and depressed mood than in recent years, and together we can raise one another up and wake up to live more fulfilling lives on purpose and with purpose.

And it's all happening for a reason—for this reason, perhaps. To wake us up. I continue to do this work myself to make sure I am maintaining some level of objective awareness and to ensure that I am not trapped by Ego in the dark and gloomy pit of despair. It is in that place where Ego can hold us hostage, reminding us of how aspects of our lives are not the way we want them or "deserve" them to be, and it is Ego who tells us why. He tells us why we are not worthy or how we messed it all up. Instead of living in that place, doesn't it feel a little better even considering the alternative? The alternative is taking back control and living life consciously and with purpose and with the ability to recognize on a daily basis that everything happens for a reason. Life is leaving us little gifts if only we are aware enough to pick them up.

Bringing It All Together

Throughout these pages, I hope that you have understood that I am a flawed person who has found a way to transform the way I live life through mindfulness, meditation, and detaching from my own egoic thoughts. With the help of my background in psychology and being a therapist in private practice, I have shared with you my own egoic interpretations and how I have used them to reflect on my own life in order to facilitate psychological healing from the tough stuff and traumatic events. My own personal journey is far from over, but in formulating the techniques and tools necessary for mental peace, I felt that it was too helpful to keep to myself.

I am still a complete mess at times. I am impulsive, and I have a wicked addiction to frozen pizza (DiGiorno Pizzaria Supreme. It's my weakness!) I have had my fair share of "bad mommy" moments and meltdowns with my daughters. I've made mistakes, some terrible mistakes, and I still make mistakes. But through the technique of recognizing egoic thoughts and detaching from them by grounding, I have been able to help myself more than years of traditional talk therapy and antidepressants combined.

I will continue to advocate for talk therapy, as I am a therapist myself. However, everyone is different, and this is an approach that I have found to be beneficial for so many individuals across a variety of ages and circumstances. These techniques involved in rewiring the way our brains interpret information are vital to improving our quality of life. Perhaps they are vital to improving the overall state of the world right now.

There is so much to be scared of and so much uncertainty in the world, and we have a choice in how we handle that. We can choose to keep our heads buried in the sand and just try to get by the way we've been getting by, or we can choose to detach from egoic thoughts by recognizing what they are, grounding ourselves in reality, and understanding what we have control over. We will always have control over how we choose to react if we are awake and aware and if we are conscious of what is actually happening, right here, right now.

If we can practice, every day, slowing down and detaching from egoic thoughts, perhaps we will find ourselves living life on purpose and with a bit less cynicism. Maybe we will explore our own defense mechanisms and their origins in order to be okay with living life consciously. Depending on where you are in your own spiritual journey, you may not really be okay with waking up. And that's not a problem. Everything happens for a reason, and maybe this stuff is going to be too much for you at first. But you'll come around to your own understanding of these techniques. Take these and make them your own. If you are awake more often than you are lost in egoic thought, that's great. If you are in control of your life more frequently than Ego is, that's wonderful. We should not be so content to live with our (Ego's interpretation) suffering. We have a responsibility to ourselves to clean up the thoughts and images in our own heads. After all, if we don't do it, who will? The easier thing to do will be to do nothing. And by doing nothing, you are giving up on yourself. Depression and anxiety may be fickle beasts, but you do not have to succumb to their will.

I've given you some perspective and my own history, in pieces, as it pertains to the effectiveness of these tools. I challenge you to try it. I own my faults and my flaws. I own my mistakes, and I hope to continue learning from them so I can stop repeating some of them. I am not better than anyone, and I would never claim to be. In my professional work, I stumbled upon a combination of simple and free techniques and tools to more effectively combat depression, anxiety, anger, and compulsive behaviors than traditional talk therapy and medication combinations. I know because I have shared with you my own struggle. I was in therapy for years, and while it felt good to vent about some problems or things on my mind, no one told me that I could take back control of those things swirling around in my mind. No, they'd suggest I see a psychiatrist and get on some meds instead. Even the psychiatrist didn't suggest anything like this; he just wrote out a prescription for medication after medication. Nothing worked, maybe because it was not 100 percent a chemical imbalance but it was Ego driving the bus! Meds aren't going to get him out of the driver's seat. We have to do it ourselves.

I definitely came close to throwing in the towel. I shared how close I came to suicide. Reflecting on it now, all the therapists just said the same thing: "You've got to stop thinking that way. I don't think you are a bad person. They don't sound like good people to spend time with. Just stop. Calm down. Try something different." No one told me that I could take control of the thoughts in my own head in order to stop perpetuating the self-deprecating thoughts that became my self-perception, self-image, and self-esteem—or lack thereof—even when my psychiatrist had me on every antidepressant and antianxiety medication that existed. I'm serious; I was on Paxil, Effexor, Prozac, Luvox, Trazodone (300 mg). If you have ever been on Trazodone, you know that, at that dose, I was taking enough to tranquilize a horse!

There were more, but I am just trying to paint a picture to show that, through all of that, no one told me anything like what I am telling you. And, honestly, even if someone had tried, I was way too lost in egoic thought to really hear them or take what they said seriously. But it all happened for a reason. I had to go through the tough stuff in order to really understand. I had to do my own work to get over the tough stuff, too. I'm not mad at some of those key players who contributed to my more challenging circumstances; it was all part of the journey. If all of that stuff hadn't happened, then maybe I wouldn't be who I am today and maybe I wouldn't be where I am today. That is way easier to say now than when I was in the thick of it.

It is with this understanding that I write what I hope will be a helpful guide toward taking back control of our own lives. I was asking for help, and I had people listen to my woes, but I felt hopeless that my depression and anxiety would ever go away. I took meds and I smoked cigarettes, all of it just adding to the incessant egoic thoughts that narrated for me how horrible I felt and how no one cared. And, more importantly, none of those things took any of the pain and suffering away. It was a maladaptive bandage that just helped me forget about it for a while. But when it all got out of my system, the pain was still there.

Now, through my own journey, I am able to remain stable more often than not. I still have slip-ups every so often, but I can be kind to myself when I recognize that I have been lost, whereas before I would be so mean to myself. I now know that only perpetuates the strength of Ego and renders me powerless in my own life. Imagine what life would be like if we all took responsibility for our thoughts and emotional reactions to them? Imagine more people living their lives consciously on purpose. How much more kind could we be toward one another? What if we were not so lost in our heads and convinced of others' disapproval of us or convinced that others are our enemies? If we can stay present in this moment, right here and right now, and remain aware of the thoughts that serve a purpose versus the thoughts that serve only to strengthen Ego, then we could actually connect to one another without fear of being judged harshly or mocked. It is our responsibility to ourselves to wake up and take action regarding the thoughts in our own heads. If not us, then who? It is up to each of us alone to raise our energy, raise our positive vibrations, and maintain them while remaining clear on who we actually are and what we really want in our lives. And when we feel out of sorts, meditate. It's that simple. Meditating in combination with grounding our thoughts can help us to remain firmly planted in reality and help the drama fall away. The beauty of a spiritual life will unfold all around us.

It's unnecessary, you see—the drama in our lives, whatever that may be moment to moment. We created it, or rather, Ego creates it to make sense of the world around us. He has all the emotions at his fingertips to show us why we are in the situation we are in and how we should feel about it when, in reality, life is offering us a lesson, a choice. When we align with Ego, we miss the lesson because we are wrapped up in the emotional or egoic interpretation of what is happening and why. If we practice remaining aware and awake, then we can accept the lesson or the challenge, and perhaps we can move through life with far fewer struggles and far less resistance.

If someone picks up this book and can get into what I'm talking about, I am optimistic that there will be a positive change. Anyone who picks up this book is doing it because they feel like something's got to give. Hopefully they are in a place to really take matters into their own hands and start using these techniques and tools to really wake up. Since you have picked up the book, you can wake up and recognize that you are not the thoughts in your head. You are not the things that have happened to you. You are not a victim of your own life. You are a truly beautiful person, and you can share that person with the world. Recognize what you have control over and don't take the negativity from others and make it your cross to bear. Maintain the mindful awareness you have achieved and know that you are awake. Those who toss their negativity and cynicism around like garbage are unconscious and "know not what they do." You own the work you have put into living a more positive, more grounded life, and no one can take that away from you. Maintain your increased level of awareness and have compassion for those who don't even know there is another way. Everything in life happens for a reason. Now is your turn to begin living life consciously with awareness and with purpose.

WORKS CITED

Freud, Sigmund. (n.d.). AZQuotes.com. Retrieved October 27, 2017, from AZQuotes.com Web site: http://www.azquotes.com/quote/846999

Recommended Reads

Epstein, Mark. *Going to Pieces Without Falling Apart.* Copyright 1998 by Mark Epstein. Broadway Books, a division of Random House, Inc., 1540 Broadway, New York, NY 10036.

Harris, Dan. *10% Happier.* Copyright 2014 by Daniel Benjamin Harris. HarperCollins Publishers, 195 Broadway, New York, NY 10007.

Redfield, James. *The Celestine Prophecy* Series. Copyright 1993 by James Redfield. Grand Central Publishing. Hachette Book Group, 1290 Avenue of the Americas, New York, NY.

Ruiz, Don Miguel. *The Four Agreements.* Copyright 2011 by Don Miguel Ruiz. Amber-Allen Publishing.

Singer, Michael. *The Surrender Experiment.* Copyright 2015 by Michael A. Singer. Harmony Books, an imprint of the Crown Publishing Group, a division of Penguin Random House LLC, New York.

Singer, Michael. *The Untethered Soul*. Copyright 2007 by Michael A. Singer. New Harbinger Publications, Inc., 5674 Shattuck Avenue Oakland, CA 94609

Tolle, Eckhart. *The Power of Now.* Copyright 1999 by Eckhart Tolle. New World Library 14 Pamaron Way Novato, CA 94949 and Namaste Publishing P.O. Box 62084 Vancouver, B.C., Canada V6J 4A3

Yogananda, Paramahansa. *Autobiography of a Yogi.* Copyright 1946 Paramahansa Yogananda. Self Realization Fellowship, 3880 San Rafael Ave., Los Angeles, CA

Printed in the United States
By Bookmasters